WITHDRAWN

# GEM OF
# THE OCEAN

1904

# GEM OF THE OCEAN

1904

## AUGUST WILSON

SERIES INTRODUCTION BY JOHN LAHR

FOREWORD BY PHYLICIA RASHAD

THEATRE COMMUNICATIONS GROUP
NEW YORK
2007

*The August Wilson Century Cycle* is funded in part by the Ford Foundation, with addi-
tional support from The Paul G. Allen Family Foundation, The Heinz Endowments
and the New York State Council on the Arts.

TCG books are exclusively distributed to the book trade by Consortium Book Sales
and Distribution, 1045 Westgate Drive, St. Paul, MN 55114.

LIBRARY OF CONGRESS CATALOGING-IN-PUBLICATION DATA
Wilson, August.
Gem of the ocean / August Wilson.—1st ed.
p. cm.—(August Wilson Century Cycle)
Foreword by Phylicia Rashad.
ISBN-13: 978-1-55936-281-8
ISBN-10: 1-55936-281-2
1. Hill District (Pittsburgh, Pa.)—Drama. 2. African American neighborhoods—
Drama. 3. African Americans—Drama. 4. Pittsburgh (Pa.)—Drama. I. Title.
PS3573.I45677G46    2007
813'.54—dc22    2007022767

Text design and composition by Lisa Govan
Slipcase and cover design by John Gall
Cover photograph by Wayne Miller/Magnum Photos
Slipcase photographs by Dana Lixenberg (author) and David Cooper

First Edition, September 2007

*To my daughters:*
*Sakina Ansari*
*Azula Carmen Wilson,*
*May the circle be unbroken*

# Series Introduction

## by John Lahr

ERROLL GARNER: "What's new, Pops?"
LOUIS ARMSTRONG: "Nothin' new. White folks still
ahead."

August Wilson liked to say that his plays were "fat
with substance." And he was right: his ten-play cycle—
Wilson wrote one for every roiling decade of the African-
American experience in the twentieth century—transforms
historical tragedy into imaginative triumph. The blues are cat-
astrophe expressed lyrically; so are Wilson's plays, which swing
with the pulse of the African-American people, as they moved,
over the decades, from property to personhood. Together,
Wilson's plays form a kind of fever chart of the unmooring
trauma of slavery. Their historical trajectory takes African-
Americans through the shock of freedom at the turn of the
century (*Gem of the Ocean*); to the reassembling of identity in
the teens (*Joe Turner's Come and Gone*); the struggle for power
in urban America in the twenties (*Ma Rainey's Black Bottom*);
the dilemma of embracing their past as slaves in the thirties

(*The Piano Lesson*); the promises made and broken to those who served in World War II (*Seven Guitars*); the fraught adaptation to the bourgeois values of the fifties (*Fences*); the stagnancy in the midst of sixties militancy (*Two Trains Running*); the disenfranchisement during the boom of the seventies and eighties (*Jitney* and *King Hedley II*); and the assimilation into the mainstream and the accompanying spiritual alienation of the nineties (*Radio Golf*).

"From the beginning, I decided not to write about historical events or the pathologies of the black community," Wilson wrote in the *New York Times* in 2000. He went on, "Instead, I wanted to present the unique particulars of black American culture as the transformation of impulse and sensibility into codes of conduct and response, into cultural rituals that defined and celebrated ourselves as men and women of high purpose. I wanted to place this culture on stage in all its richness and fullness and to demonstrate its ability to sustain us in all areas of human life and endeavour and through profound moments of our history in which the larger society has thought less of us than we have thought of ourselves."

"The average, struggling, nonmorbid Negro is the best kept secret in America," Zora Neale Hurston wrote in 1950. Wilson's plays brought that nonmorbid Negro—his songs, his idiom, his superstitions, his homilies, his folly, his struggle—onto the stage. Wilson took the vernacular rhythms and the swaggering sludge of street talk and turned that tatterdemalion into eloquence: "A nigger with a gun is bad news," the restaurant philosopher Holloway riffs in *Two Trains Running*. "You say the word 'gun' in the same sentence with the word 'nigger' and you in trouble. The white man panic. Unless you say, 'The policeman shot the nigger with his gun.'"

For Wilson's characters, life is hard but fun isn't. The plays show high spirits as a form of heroics; the inventive energy that Wilson's characters bring to the downtime of their stalled days only underscores the waste of their talent. Wilson has written a social history of his times, not an economic one; it is all the more profound and persuasive because it teaches through joy, not reason. With their gorgeous fuss, his characters bear witness to what Wilson, in the first lines of *Ma Rainey's Black Bottom*, called the black man's "dazed and dazzling . . . rapport with life": they dance the Juba ( *Joe Turner's Come and Gone*); they reenact the hoodoo of ancient ritual (*Gem of the Ocean*); they do the "Joe Louis Victory Walk" (*Seven Guitars*); they beat out field chants (*The Piano Lesson*) and they sing the blues (*Ma Rainey's Black Bottom*). The noise the characters make and the time their tall tales take are redress for what Zora Neale Hurston called "the muteness of slavery."

"Blacks in America want to forget slavery—the stigma, the shame," Wilson told the *New York Times* in 1987. "That's the wrong move. If you can't be who you are, who can you be?" Wilson's theatrical mission—unique in his time—was, he said, "about reclaiming those things which were lost during slavery." When he was growing up, in the Hill District of Pittsburgh, in the late forties and fifties, his parents used to admonish him, "Don't go out there and show your color." Wilson dedicated his life and his art to doing just that: making a spectacle of blackness. No other theatrical African-American testament has been so popular, so poetic or so penetrating. "It's August's language—the rhythm of hurt, the rhythm of pain, the rhythm of ecstasy, the rhythm of family—which sets him apart, and is why we call him the heavyweight champion," said Marion McClinton, who directed some later productions of Wilson's plays.

"Daddy, why you a writer?" Wilson's young daughter, Azula, once asked him. "To tell the story," he said. He wanted African-Americans to hold their past in their present, to have their race's losses inform their gains. He saw himself as a warrior. "As men, we are charged with the defense of the race, of the ethnic tribes of our genetic marrow," he wrote. "We are charged with propagation and we are charged with the advancement of prosperity. But where as men do we find sustenance?" He gave back to black audiences the experience of themselves (and to white audiences, an understanding of that experience). His plays, in their mythological overtones and narrative style, capture not just the African dialect but the African idiom; his strategic storytelling maps the ceremonies, the triumphs and the emptiness of the dispossessed African-American heart. As Ma Rainey says of the blues, Wilson's cycle takes that emptiness and tries to "fill it up with something."

Deprived of their history, their language, their education, their family structure, their access to capital, even their gods, African-Americans post-slavery were strangers both to themselves and to American abundance. According to Wilson, they had no moral personality, and no moral status in civic and church law. Black men are "a commodity of flesh and muscle which has lost its value in the marketplace," Wilson wrote. They are "left over from history." In *Ma Rainey's Black Bottom*, this phrase is repeated and expanded on by Toledo, a session musician. "The problem ain't with the white man," he says to Levee, a go-getting black trumpeter who believes that the bubble of the twenties is within his grasp. "The white man knows you just a leftover. 'Cause he the one who done the eating and he know what he done ate. But we don't know that we been took and made history out of. Done went and filled the white man's belly and now he's full and tired and wants you to get out the way and let him be by himself."

Freedom, once African-Americans finally achieved it, proved a perilous undertaking. "You on an adventure, Mr. Citizen," Aunt Ester says in *Gem of the Ocean*, to Citizen Barlow, so named because he was born a free man. "I bet you didn't know that. It's all adventure. You signed up for it and didn't even know it." Later, the old runaway slave and activist Solly Two Kings, who makes his living collecting and selling dog shit for leatherworking and fertilizer, says to Barlow, "It's hard to be a citizen. You gonna have to fight to get that. And time you get it you be surprised how heavy it is." What was supposed to be Heaven for African-Americans turned into another form of Hell. "The people think they in freedom," Solly says. "I say I got it but what is it? I'm still trying to find out. It ain't never been nothing but trouble . . . All it mean is you got a long row to hoe and ain't got no plow. Ain't got no seed. Ain't got no mule. What good is freedom if you can't do nothing with it?"

"What one begs the American people to do, for all our sakes, is simply to accept our history," James Baldwin wrote in his essay, "The American Dream and the American Negro." But what was that heritage, and what was the psychic price paid for subjugation? The answer, as Wilson dramatized it, is as hard to fathom for blacks as it is for whites. In *Gem of the Ocean*, for instance, Citizen Barlow doesn't know anything about the Civil War. History is lost on him. Of the many impoverishments of the African-American, perhaps the most pernicious is that his loss of the past left him no way to make sense of his present. In Wilson's cycle, this mutation of memory—a sort of chronic cultural amnesia—echoes down the decades.

Aunt Ester, central to many of the plays, is the antidote to this malaise. A two-hundred-and-eighty-five-year-old conjure woman at the beginning of the cycle, she is the embodiment of African-American wisdom, tradition and folklore—what Zora Neale Hurston called "the boiled-down juice of human living." Aunt Ester is the repository of "the blood's memory" as Wilson often called it; she contains, he said, the "valuable tools for the reconstruction of their personality and . . . for exposing all the places where [society] is lacking in virtue." The cycle opens, in *Gem*, with Citizen Barlow pounding on Aunt Ester's front door at 1839 Wylie—an address that has become as iconic in American dramatic literature as Grover's Corners. (The cycle ends, in *Radio Golf*, with Aunt Ester all but forgotten and her residence now slated for demolition.) Barlow, who feels "like I got a hole inside me," has heard that Aunt Ester "washes souls." Through her intercessions, he makes spiritual contact with the City of Bones—the world's largest unmarked graveyard—where many of his ancestors were left while being transported in chains to the New World. Barlow emerges from this imaginative submersion into his historical past with a sense of purpose, "all filled up inside."

Even when Aunt Ester is not invoked, this reconnection, a sort of respiritualization, is central to the drama in many of Wilson's plays. In *The Piano Lesson*, for instance, the story of slavery is carved into the piano that Boy Willie comes North from Mississippi to reclaim from his sister, Berniece, so that he can finance the purchase of a farm. Berniece wants to hold on to the piano and the family story it tells. "All that's in the past," Boy Willie tells their uncle. "If my daddy had seen where he could have traded that piano in for some land of his own, it wouldn't be sitting up here now." Wilson's personal belief was that it was a mistake for African-Americans to leave the South. "The blood and bones of two hundred and fifty years of our ancestors are buried in the South, and we came North," he told me. "I think if we'd stayed South and continued to empower ourselves, in terms of acquiring land—we already had acres of farmland that we owned—we'd have had ten black senators in the United States. We'd be represented. We'd be a more culturally secure and culturally self-sufficient people." *The Piano Lesson* circles around this historical conundrum. The battle between Berniece and her brother, which seems to be about the ownership of property, is, in fact, about the ownership of spiritual continuity.

Wilson's characters are sometimes as incurious about themselves as the white man is. In *Ma Rainey*, Toledo, the only musician in the band who can read, observes his friends with an anthropological eye: "That's African," he says, of a fellow musician's rhetorical turn of phrase. Slow Drag, the bass player, replies, "Nigger, I ain't no African! I ain't doing no African nothing!" The comedy and caricature of the exchanges—"You don't see me running around in no jungle with no bone between my nose," Levee chips in—serves to indicate just how estranged the musicians are from their own origins. They don't have their cultural bearings, and this internal vacancy manifests itself in a way of being—a rudderlessness—that only adds to their unexamined grief. When they rehearse, the trombonist, Cutler, repeatedly counts the band in with the phrase "One . . . two . . . You know what to do." But, other than playing their instruments, the musicians *don't* know what to do; they are flummoxed by their own impotence and ignorance.

Prowess and stasis are among the galling, poignant contradictions with which many of Wilson's characters contend. In *Seven Guitars*, for instance, Floyd "Schoolboy" Barton has a hit blues record and a contract waiting for him in Chicago; he just doesn't have the wherewithal to get his guitar out of hock. In *Fences*, the braggart Troy Maxson cuts a figure as heroic as that of Charley Burley, the Hall of Fame fighter who was Wilson's Pittsburgh neighbor and who, like Maxson, lived out his later days as a garbageman. Maxson, a great baseball player who came along too early to play in the integrated major leagues— "There ought not never have been no time called too early!" he says—wants to win a promotion as the first black garbage-truck driver, but he can't read to get his license.

Maxson is one of many Wilson characters—Floyd Barton, Boy Willie, Levee and Ma Rainey among them—who celebrate themselves through style; in their attitude and self-presentation, it's as if, Wilson wrote, "They might transform and forever enlarge the possibilities that might exist. They might by sheer power of their presence, enlarge their universe." Take, for instance, Levee and his new Florsheim shoes, which are for him totems of urban mobility and promise: "A man got to have some shoes to dance like this!" he says. "You can't dance like this with them clodhoppers Toledo got." But the almost symphonic display of defiant personality is frequently counterpointed in the plays by a show of demented absence. The deranged, driven crazy by disappointment, have a prophetic place in Wilson's imaginary communities. In *Fences*, Gabriel Maxson, Troy's brother, who had half his brain blown out in World War II and now thinks he is the archangel Gabriel, embodies a living death that his brother struggles against. In *Two Trains Running*, Hambone, having been given a chicken instead of the promised ham as payment for painting a local butcher's fence, embarks on a simple-minded obsessive lament—"I want my ham. He gonna give me my ham"— which becomes an anthem to the white world's racist caprice.

These demented characters are in the grip, as Wilson wrote of Gabriel, of "a trauma that a sane and normal mind would be unable to withstand." Their witness works in the plays as the "fools" do in Shakespeare; they say the unsayable. In *Seven Guitars*, for instance, Hedley speaks in riddles and dreams out loud, claiming his inheritance as some kind of king or leader. "Everybody say Hedley crazy," he says of himself. "Because he know the place of the black man is not at the foot of the white man's boot." At one point, after some comic grousing about a neighbor's rooster, Hedley bolts from his yard to return the offending piece of poultry. "God ain't making no more roosters," he declares. "It is a thing past. Soon you mark my words when God ain't making no more niggers. They too be a done thing." He wrings the chicken's neck. It's a shocking moment. "Hedley's whole warning is, 'If the rooster has become useless, then what about you? Maybe you'll become useless, too,'" Wilson told me. "If you don't connect to the past, then you don't know who you are in the present. You may prove to be unworthy of the past."

. . .

Although Wilson's stories involve the occasional Caucasian emissary—Rutherford Selig, the charming peddler and People Finder (*Gem of the Ocean* and *Joe Turner's Come and Gone*); Sturdyvant and Irvin, the recording studio executives (*Ma Rainey*)—the white world as a whole remains a primarily invisible but palpable presence, pressing in on the characters and changing the flow of things. "I look around and say, 'Where the barbed wire?'" King says in *King Hedley II*, observing that as a slave he would have been worth twelve hundred dollars, and now he's worth only three dollars and thirty-five cents an hour. "They got everything else. They got me blocked in every other way. 'Where the barbed wire?'" To which his sidekick, Mister, replies, "If they had some barbed wire you could cut through it. But you can't cut through not having no job."

"Blacks know the spiritual truth of white America," Wilson told me. "We're living examples of America's hypocrisy. We know white America better than white America knows us." Sometimes in Wilson's tales the white presence is embodied by African-Americans themselves, adopting the energy and ideas of their oppressors. In *Radio Golf*, set at the end of the century, Pittsburgh's Hill District is in the process of being redeveloped by African-Americans who finally have access to some mainstream power and money, but their idiom and their concerns have lost all connection to their roots. The talk is of golf, not justice. "I hit my first golf ball I asked myself where have I been?" Roosevelt Hicks, one of the black developers, says. "I watched the ball soar down the driving range . . . I felt like the world was open to me. Everything and everybody." However, for most of Wilson's characters, the white world is not an aspiration but an impediment; they are constantly thrown up against the whims of its authority. In *Ma Rainey*, a music producer reneges on his promise to record Levee's arrangements; in *Two Trains Running*, when the jailbird Sterling plays the numbers and finally wins, the white syndicate shrinks the odds and the payout. "Poor folks can't get nothing,"

Rose says in *Fences*. The characters struggle under the weight of white ownership and the absence of capital. "The thrust of integration and the lack of a relationship to banking capital meant that we could not continue to develop the economic base that we'd begun," Wilson told me.

Necessity is the ozone of Wilson's dramas. His characters do the math, but nothing adds up. Troy Maxson can't get credit; Seth Holly (*Joe Turner's Come and Gone*) can't get a loan to expand his hardware business; Youngblood (*Jitney*) can't get the down payment to buy a home; Floyd "Schoolboy" Barton has a record contract in hand but not a penny in his pocket—he gets put in jail for ninety days and charged with "worthlessness": "I don't want to live my life without," he says. "Everybody I know live without. I don't want to do that. I want to live with." In *Gem of the Ocean*, Citizen Barlow has to pay his entire wages for room and board to the mill that hires him: he can't afford to live or to leave. "Making the people owe is worse than slavery," he says. In *Two Trains Running*, Sterling tries to sell his watch to get a stake: "Seventeen jewels!" he says. "And I can't get five dollars for it." Roosevelt Hicks, in *Radio Golf*, can crunch the numbers—"I figured I'd ask for fifteen, take twelve, and adjust my ownership allowance so it can accrue up to twenty-five percent"—but his language, like his soul, is dead. Holloway says at one point in *Two Trains Running*, "People kill me talking about niggers is lazy. Niggers is the most hardworking people in the world. Worked three hundred years for free. And didn't take no lunch hour."

The prospect of profit seems to be the only thing that can overcome the white world's indifference to African-Americans. "Look at that. 'Mr. Floyd Barton,'" Floyd says to his girlfriend, showing off his letter from Savoy Records. "You get you a hit record and the white folks call you Mister." Ma Rainey, who is not "spooked up with the white men," understands the law of economics behind such punctilio; it emboldens her to make the white record executives dance to her tune. "If you colored and can make them some money, then you all right with them," she says. "Otherwise, you just a dog in the alley." When she enters the recording studio, she enters with demands: she wants her car to be fixed, her stuttering nephew to perform on the record, Coca-Colas to be supplied during her session, and her tempos to be kept. The white management hops to it. Rainey, a character who doesn't give up anything but bubble gum and hard times, takes a lot of oxygen out of the room; her queenliness is as much an act of psychological revenge for the second-class citizenship inflicted on African-Americans as it is a show of earning power. "What you all say don't count with me," she tells the producers. "Ma listens to her heart. Ma listens to the voice inside her." Her accomplishment is not wealth but identity. She pronounces herself in the world. An African-American solo singer was a comparatively new and extremely potent phenomenon in the twenties. Wilson, speaking of singers like Rainey who included their names in their lyrics, told me, "There's something wonderful about that. They're making a stand. They're saying, 'This is me. This is what I have to say.'" The real Ma Rainey, who is often referred to as "the mother of the blues," always used quotation marks around her first name in print and on record labels. Wilson, for his stage appropriation of her life, removed the punctuation and also the implied irony. To the white producers, who packaged Rainey's sound on cheap, poorly mastered records, the "Ma" was hyperbolic. ("I'm not putting up with any Royal Highness . . . Queen of the Blues bullshit," Sturdyvant says, near the beginning of the play.) To the black world, Rainey's outspoken popular music—with its combination of cynicism, sorrow and sass—offered warmth, as well as redress; it made her both a mother and a kind of priestess, "a celebrant," as Ralph Ellison called Rainey's protégée and competitor Bessie Smith, "who affirmed the values of the group and man's ability to deal with chaos." Wilson's Rainey may look to the white world for her money, but not for her validation. "White folks don't understand about the blues," she says. "They hear it come out, but . . . don't understand that's life's way of talking. You don't sing to feel better. You sing 'cause that's a way of understanding life."

Wilson himself didn't discover the blues until his early twenties. At a thrift shop in the St. Vincent de Paul charity shop in the Hill, he bought a bootleg 78-rpm record on whose tattered yellow label he could make out the words: "Bessie Smith: 'Nobody in Town Can Bake a Sweet Jelly Roll Like Mine.'" Smith's impudent, unabashed sound stunned him. "The universe stuttered and everything fell to a new place," he wrote later. The moment was an epiphany for him: "a birth, a baptism and a redemption all rolled up in one," he said. Wilson played the song twenty-two times straight. "Then I started laughing, you know, 'cause it suddenly dawned on me that there was another record on the other side," he told me.

The discovery would have a profound influence on his writing. "I take the same approach as a bluesman, the same ideas and attitudes," he told me in 1996. "For instance, lines that say, 'I'm leavin' this mornin', I'm gonna start out walkin', and take a chance I may ride' is your whole world view." He added, "When the old folks sang, 'Everything's gonna be all right,' it *was* all right, simply because they sang. They made it all right by their singing. They just changed their attitudes. The blues emboldened them to survive whatever the circumstance was." The blues, he explained, "made me look at the word differently. It gave the people in the rooming house where I lived, and also my mother, a history I didn't know they had. It was the beginning of my consciousness that I was the carrier of some very valuable antecedents."

Wilson's pedigree was complicated. He was born Frederick August Kittel, in 1945, the first son and the fourth of six children born to Fritz Kittel, a white immigrant German baker, and Daisy Wilson, his African-American wife. Fritz was drunken, abusive and distant; Wilson inherited his father's fierce temper and wrote their bumptious relationship into the obdurate father-son battles of *Jitney* and *Fences*. By the time Wilson was twenty and had taken up his own residence in the Hill, he had dropped out of high school, read his way through the local library, fought with his disappointed mother, joined the Army, worked in a pharmacy, and buried his mostly unmourned father. His best friend in those early days was a street hustler turned poet called Chawley Williams. "August wasn't really black. He was half-and-half," Williams said. "He was too dark to be white, and he was too white to be dark. He was in no man's land. I knew he was lost. I was lost. Kindred brothers know one another. We were trying to become men. We didn't even know what it meant." In time, through his plays, Wilson would write himself into the center of modern black American history. But when he hit the streets at twenty he had no money, no marketable skills, no proven talent. He was, he said, "searching for something you can claim as yours."

The African-American community embraced him, nurtured him, educated him, and contained his rage at his father's abandonment. "He's so faithful to the blackness," the actor James Earl Jones, who starred in the Broadway production of *Fences*, told me. "He's faithful like a father—that represents fidelity to him." Once Wilson discovered the blues he became convinced that he was somehow "the conduit of ancestors." Whenever a local died and was mourned at West's Funeral Home, on the Hill, Wilson felt compelled—for personal reasons, not for art's sake—to go and pay his respects, regardless of whether he had ever met the deceased. "I felt that this is a life that has gone before me," he explained. From Claude McKay's book *Home to Harlem*, he learned of a cigar store and pool hall in his own neighborhood called Pat's Place, where a lot of community elders congregated. Pat's Place became his Oxford, and its garrulous denizens—"walking history books,"

Wilson called them—his professors. They called him Young-blood. "I was just like, 'Hey, man, how did you get to be so old, 'cause it's hard out here.' I really wanted to know how they survived. 'How do you get to be seventy years old in America?'"

One old-timer at Pat's Place told Wilson, "I been watchin' you . . . You carrying around a ten-gallon bucket. You carry that ten-gallon bucket through life, and you gon' always be disappointed . . . Get you a little cup. Carry that through life. And that way, if somebody put a little bit in it, why, you got sumpn." Wilson told me, "I managed to cut it down to a gallon bucket, but I never did get that little cup." Wilson always thought big; his grandiosity as a teenager earned him the nickname "Napoleon." "My mother made me believe that I could do anything," he said. "I wanted to be the best at whatever I did. I was the best dishwasher in Pittsburgh. I really was. I got a raise the first day I was there. When I sit down to write, I want to write the best play that's ever been written. Sometimes that's a fearsome place to stand, but that's when you call on your courage." April 1, 1964 was the day that Wilson began drawing on his courage: he walked to downtown Pittsburgh, put twenty dollars on a counter of a pawnshop, and came away with the heavy black Royal Standard that he'd noticed on display in the window. He had decided to reinvent himself in the heroic mold of the poet. "What I discovered is that writing was the only thing society would allow me to do," he told me. "I couldn't have a job or be a lawyer because I didn't do all the things necessary. What I was allowed to do was write. If they saw me over in the corner scribbling on a piece of paper they would say: 'That is just a nigger over in the corner scribbling on a piece of paper.' Nobody said, 'Hey, you can't do that.' So I felt free."

Most sightings of Wilson in those days took place in restaurants—the White Tower, the B & W, Moose's, Eddie's—where he was bent over, scribbling on his tablet or on napkins. Decades later, he'd walk through the neighborhood and people would stop him and ask, "You still drawin'?" "I found out later people thought I was a bum," he told me. "The thing that sustained me was that my idea of myself was different from the idea that society, my mother, and even some of my friends had of me. I saw myself as a grand person." He went on, "I saw the pictures of Richard Wright, Langston Hughes—all of them always had a suit on. I thought, Yeah, that's me. I want to be like that." At a thrift shop, he bought white shirts for a dime, the broad ties he favored for a nickel and sport coats for thirty-five cents. He had come under the influence of Dylan Thomas's poetry, and he lived through the Black Power movement with a coat and tie and a pipe, intoning poetry with an English accent. "People thought he was crazy in the neighborhood," Chawley Williams said.

Wilson published his first poem in 1969, but, by his own admission, he didn't achieve his poetic voice ("surety—the line burned in the hand," he called it, quoting the poet Robert Duncan) until 1973, eight years after his first rejection from *Harper's* in 1964. Then, on March 5, 1978 Wilson left the Hill and moved to St. Paul, Minnesota. There he married his second wife, Judith Oliver, a white social worker. (His first wife, Brenda Burton, is the mother of his eldest daughter, Sakina.) He went from a neighborhood that had fifty-five thousand blacks to an entire state that had the same number. "There weren't many black folks around," he told me. "In that silence, I could hear the language for the first time." Until then, he said, he hadn't "valued or respected the way that black folks talked. I'd always thought that in order to create art out of it you had to change that," he said. Now he missed the street talk and wanted to preserve it. "I got lonely and missed those guys," he said. "I could hear the music."

When he began to write plays, Wilson claimed, he "couldn't write dialogue." His early experiments leaned toward the florid and artistic. In one early dramatic experiment, in which a man and a woman talk on a park bench, the woman says, "Terror hangs over the night like a hawk." At least one of the plays that

Wilson wrote in this stilted language—*The Coldest Day of the Year*—was produced. "It wasn't black American language," he said. It wasn't theater either. Years before, Wilson had asked a Pittsburgh friend and playwright, Rob Penny, "How do you make characters talk?" "You don't," Penny said. "You listen to them."

In 1979, Wilson sat down at Arthur Treacher's Fish & Chips, a restaurant up the street from his apartment in St. Paul, to write a play to submit to The O'Neill Playwrights Conference, a conference held at a sprawling estate in Waterford, Connecticut, where each summer about a dozen playwrights are provided with a dramaturg, a director and a cast to help them explore their flawed but promising plays. The play that Wilson submitted was *Jitney*. As he conjured up the Pittsburgh taxi stand that was one of his former hangouts, Wilson recalled Penny's advice. He listened to his characters and let them speak—he finished the play in ten days. "I found that exhilarating," he said. "It felt like this was what I'd been looking for, something that was mine, that would enable me to say anything." For Wilson, the revelation was that, quoting the African leader Ahmed Sékou Touré, "'language describes the idea of the one who speaks it'; so if I'm speaking the oppressor's language I'm in essence speaking his ideas too. This is why I think blacks speak their own language, because they have to find another way." Writing *Jitney* proved to Wilson that he didn't have to reconstitute black life; he just had to capture it.

The O'Neill rejected *Jitney*. Its incredulous author, assuming that no one had read it, submitted the play again. The O'Neill rejected it again. Wilson took serious stock of his newfound calling. His inner dialogue, he told me, was: "'maybe it's not as good as you think. You have to write a better play.' 'I've already written the best play I can write.' 'Why don't you write above your talent?' 'Oh, man, how can you do that?' 'Well, you can write beneath it, can't you?' 'Oh, yeah.'" Wilson turned back to a play on Ma Rainey that he'd begun a year earlier and began to imagine it differently. "I opened up the door to the band room," he said. "Slow Drag and Cutler were talking about how Slow Drag got his name. Then this guy walked in— he had glasses, carrying the books—he became Toledo. I had discovered them and got them talking." Wilson, whose focused gaze could bring his characters to uncanny, sometimes awesome life, was not much influenced or inhibited by the canon of Western Theater for the simple reason that he had not read or seen any of it. (With the exception of his own plays, and a few by his friends, at the time we spoke in 2001, Wilson claimed to have seen only about a dozen plays.) "I consider it a blessing that when I started writing plays in earnest, in 1979, I had not read Chekhov. I hadn't read Ibsen. I hadn't read Tennessee Williams, Arthur Miller, or O'Neill." It had taken him eight years of reading and writing to find his voice in poetry. "I didn't want to take eight years to find my voice as a playwright," he said.

*Ma Rainey's Black Bottom*, which opened in 1984, was only the second African-American play to be produced on Broadway; the first was Lorraine Hansberry's 1959 *A Raisin in the Sun*. Lloyd Richards, whom Wilson later called "my guide, my mentor and my provocateur," directed them both. Richards, who was head of the Yale Drama School, as well as the artistic director of The O'Neill, guided Wilson's talent from obscurity directly into the mainstream. (Ben Mordecai, then the managing director of the Yale Repertory Theatre, would become Wilson's business partner and co-producer.) From *Ma Rainey's Black Bottom* to *Seven Guitars*, all of Wilson's plays would follow the same golden path: from The O'Neill to Yale to regional theaters to Broadway. Richards asserted his quiet control from the first rehearsal of *Ma Rainey* at the Yale Repertory Theatre in 1984. "We go into the room with the actors, we read the play," Wilson recalled. "An actor had a question about a character. I started to speak, and Lloyd answered the question. There was another question, and Lloyd answered it again. I remember there was a moment when I thought, The old fox knows what's going on. This is gonna be Okay." "We had a pattern of work," Richards said of their partnership, which in time would become as influential as that of Tennessee Williams and Elia Kazan. "I would work on it, check it with him, so I included him, but I was the director." Richards added, "August was very receptive in the early days. He had a lot to learn and knew it. He was a big sponge, absorbing everything." Richards sent him to the sound booth, to the paint shop, to the lighting designer. "As he learned structure—playwriting, really—he was also learning everything else," Richards said. In time, with producer Ben Mordecai, Wilson formed his own production company— Sageworks—to produce his own work. (Richards died in 2006, at the age of eighty-seven.)

From 1994 to the end of his life, Wilson lived in Seattle and worked in the crepuscular gloom of the low-ceilinged basement of his house, lit by bars of neon, where he went to sneak cigarettes, listen to music, and wait for his characters to arrive. His writing method was improvisational; he likened it to the collages of Romare Bearden, one of his artistic heroes. "I just started with a line of dialogue or with a feeling," he told Suzan-Lori Parks in *American Theatre* magazine in 2005, shortly before he died of cancer at the age of sixty. "I just write stuff down and pile it up, and when I get enough stuff I spread it out and look at it and figure out how to use it . . . You start to build the scene and you don't know where the scene's going." He went on, "You shift [things] around and organize it . . . until you have a composition that satisfies you, that expresses the idea of something and then—bingo—you have a play." Wilson's process took patience, confidence and courage. He had begun his extraordinary endeavor well into his late thirties, and he did not spend his time on the telephone or watching television or going to the movies. (Between 1980 and 1991, he saw only two films, both directed by Martin Scorsese—*Raging Bull* and *Cape Fear*.)

Wilson approached each day's writing with ritualistic rigor. "I wash my hands," he told me. "I always want to say I approached it with clean hands—you know, a symbolic cleansing."

Wilson wrote standing up, at a high, cluttered accounting desk, where he propped his legal pad, and then transferred his jottings to a laptop computer. For years, an Everlast punching bag was suspended from the ceiling about two steps behind his writing table. When Wilson was in full flow and the dialogue was popping, he'd stop, pivot, throw a barrage of punches at the bag, then turn back to work. (When I visited him, while he was rewriting *King Hedley II*, he had recently knocked down the bag and its ceiling hook.) Pinned on a bulletin board just beside where he stood when writing were two quotations, as bold as street signs: TAKE IT TO THE MOON (Frank Gehry) and DON'T BE AFRAID. JUST PLAY THE MUSIC (Charlie Parker). I called him in 2005, just before the Yale opening of *Radio Golf*, to ask what it felt like, after twenty-four years of single-minded striving, to finish the final installment of his cycle. Wilson said that while he was writing *Radio Golf*, he had listened to Three Dog Night's "The Show Must Go On." One line in particular had stuck in his head: "I wish maybe they'd tear down the walls of this theater and let me out." "That's the way I felt," he said.

August Wilson died on October 2, 2005. "I've lived a blessed life," he said. "I'm ready." Between the diagnosis, in mid-June, and his death, he had enough time to finish the rewrites of *Radio Golf*, and set up the usual gestation period of out-of-town productions before the Broadway opening—a unique system that Wilson, Richards and his producing partner, Ben Mordecai, had set up as a kind of quality control. Wilson also lived long enough to learn that he would be the first African-American to have a Broadway theater named after him. No one else—not even Eugene O'Neill, who set out in the mid-thirties to write a nine-play cycle and managed only two—had aimed so high and achieved so much. Wilson's plays brought blacks and whites together under the same roof to share in the profound mysteries of race and class and the bittersweet awareness of how separate yet indivisible we really are.

*John Lahr has been the senior drama critic at the* New Yorker *since 1992. Among his nineteen books are* Notes on a Cowardly Lion: The Biography of Bert Lahr *and* Prick Up Your Ears: The Biography of Joe Orton. *In 2001, he spent four months interviewing August Wilson for a profile which was later republished in his book* Honky Tonk Parade: New Yorker Profiles of Show People.

# FOREWORD

*by Phylicia Rashad*

THERE IS MUCH TO BE SAID about August Wilson. In him we find the rare combination of poet, playwright, philosopher, historian, humanitarian, musician and spiritual seeker. These attributes culminate in August Wilson's *Gem of the Ocean*, making it more than just a play. It is a hymn in praise of freedom and moral redemption, an ode to community, a song of love, a wellspring of wisdom, and a summons to critical thought and action.

In our first meeting to discuss my possible involvement with the role of Aunt Ester in *Gem of the Ocean*, August explained that Aunt Ester was mentioned in previous plays (*Two Trains Running, Seven Guitars* and *King Hedley II*), because he "had heard the characters speak of her." Yet she did not appear in these plays because he had not yet heard *her* speak. One day while sitting in Eddie's, the restaurant in Pittsburgh's Hill District that he frequented, he finally heard her speak. He said, "She said she couldn't talk about the water, but the water was all she talked about." He began writing on napkins, capturing everything he heard her say. Then he picked up his cell phone, dialed his home phone and recorded his writing on the messenger service. Thinking that it could somehow be erased or lost, he proceeded to the nearest pay phone, dialed his cell number, and recorded the writing on *that* messenger service. "This," he said, "was the beginning of *Gem of the Ocean.*" He would later refer to this masterwork as "the jewel of the cycle—the mother of all the plays."

My first observation of August Wilson was that he was a man of purpose, specificity and deliberation. When we listen as *carefully* as he did, we discern meaning in every aspect of his work: the number above Aunt Ester's door (1839) refers to the Underground Railroad; the name of the character "Solly Two Kings" conveys David, the Warrior, and Solomon, the Wise; there's Ester, Citizen and Caesar (to explain everything would rob the reader of his or her own adventure, and that I will not do).

The time is 1904 and, as Caesar Wilks says, "Industry is what drive the country." It is the year of the invention of the portable typewriter, the Caterpillar tractor and the teabag. The New York subway system opens, the first tunnel beneath the Hudson River is completed, and construction begins on the Panama Canal. America, though still a young nation, has become an empire with borders extending westward to the Pacific Coast, with the purchase of Alaska from Russia, and with a military presence in Central America and in the Philippines. Forty-one years have passed since the signing of the Emancipation Proclamation, thirty-six years since the ratification of the Fourteenth Amendment. Booker T. Washington has dined at the White House as a guest of President Theodore Roosevelt, W.E.B. DuBois enjoys the celebrity of his published work *The Souls of Black Folk*, yet a vast number of descendants of Africans in America—"the people," as the characters of *Gem* call them—grapple with the question of freedom. A generation has come through slavery, another generation is born shortly after Emancipation. What does it mean to be free? Black people are denied the right to vote by the Supreme Court, as it upholds discrimination in voting registration. Jim Crow laws are in effect from Louisiana to New Hampshire. In an effort to stem the tide of black migration to Northern industrialized cities, federal authorities issue a mandate directing blacks to remain in the South and work with former slaveholders to rebuild it. As Solly says, "The people . . . got the law tied to their toe. Every time they try and swim the law pull them under."

Of those who manage the trip North, many find themselves in distress. Lacking financial resources, with little or no formal education, these recently freed slaves are forced into menial labor at the lowest wages. They live in overcrowded, rundown rooming houses or beneath bridges or anywhere else they can find. Having to purchase goods and necessities from company stores owned by the mills and factories that employ them, they are unable to break the cycle of poverty and debt. Still they come. They come with hope and faith in America's promise—Democracy: ". . . the same right to life . . . The same right to whatever there was in life they could find useful," says Black Mary.

Citizen Barlow is such a person. Our story begins with his desperate knock at the door of 1839 Wylie Avenue—Aunt Ester's house. He is troubled in mind and spirit, and the people say, "Go see Aunt Ester and get your soul washed." In entering this house of sanctuary, he will enter the experience of a new community. He will encounter a king who walks around "picking up dog shit" as he "lives [life] for the people"; a caretaker, unswerving in faith and devotion; a young woman, who, while living in this "peaceful house," is still conflicted by unfulfilled desire and indecision; a boss man who knows "the value of family" but mistakes his role and responsibility to the people; an outsider who enjoys inclusion by virtue of his honest and respectful interaction and frequent visits; and Aunt Ester, a two-hundred-and-eighty-five-year-old wise woman who serves as spiritual advisor to the community.

Citizen is on an adventure that is beyond his imagining. The washing of his soul is a spiritual journey that demands his full participation. Guided by the wisdom of Aunt Ester, he will relive the terror of the Middle Passage. In the dark night of his soul, he will come face to face with himself and acknowledge his past—the past that lives in his conscious memory, the past which is forgotten. Through remembrance and recognition of all that has gone before, he will "come to stand in the light" and be reborn as a "man of the people."

To perform a masterpiece is indeed a privilege. To work with the one who has created it is a transformative experience. I watched in amazement as August worked to refine that which I considered perfection from the start. He would enter the rehearsal hall, exchange greetings with director and cast, and take his seat. As rehearsal progressed, he would close his eyes and appear to be sleeping. After a time his eyes would open, he would rise from his seat and leave the hall. Upon his return the next day, a story previously told in a page and a half of poetic monologue now was contained in a single phrase— completely. How did he do that? He wasn't sleeping. He was listening, listening to the words, seeing the pictures they painted and feeling the rhythms produced by their combinations. He understood the power of sound and rhythm inherent in words, speech and music. He worked in alignment with that power.

As an actor, I became increasingly sensitive to these rhythms and aware of their importance. August's characters are defined by speech—the rhythms of speech serve as emotional building blocks that support the progressive movement of the play. If a word is changed or a phrase interpolated, the rhythms are altered but never to the good.

August Wilson's *Gem of the Ocean* is like a great and mighty ship riding the waves of history. With sails at full mast, blown by the winds of clarity and tireless resolve, it surges onward toward its charted destination, the port of right understanding: "So Live!"

*Phylicia Rashad is a stage, television and film actor. She received a Tony nomination for her role as Aunt Ester in the Broadway production of* Gem of the Ocean.

# GEM OF
# THE OCEAN

1904

PRODUCTION HISTORY

*Gem of the Ocean* premiered on April 28, 2003, at The Good-man Theatre (Robert Falls, Artistic Director; Roche Schulfer, Executive Director) in Chicago. The director was Marion McClinton and the consulting producer was Benjamin Mordecai; the set design was by David Gallo, the costume design was by Constanza Romero, the lighting design was by Donald Holder, the sound design was by Michael Bodeen and Rob Milburn, the music and musical direction were by Dwight Andrews; the production stage manager was Joseph Drummond and the stage managers were Narda Alcorn and T. Paul Lynch. The cast was as follows:

| | |
|---|---|
| ELI | Paul Butler |
| CITIZEN BARLOW | Kenny Leon |
| AUNT ESTER | Greta Oglesby |
| BLACK MARY | Yvette Ganier |
| RUTHERFORD SELIG | Raynor Scheine |
| SOLLY TWO KINGS | Anthony Chisholm |
| CAESAR | Peter Jay Fernandez |

The play was produced on July 20, 2003, at Center Theatre Group's Mark Taper Forum (Gordon Davidson, Artistic Director; Charles Dillingham, Managing Director) in Los Angeles. The director was Marion McClinton and the consulting producer was Benjamin Mordecai; the set design was by David Gallo, the costume design was by Constanza Romero, the lighting design was by Donald Holder, the sound design was by Dan Moses Schreier and the music was composed and arranged by Kathryn Bostic. The cast was as follows:

| | |
|---|---|
| ELI | Al White |
| CITIZEN BARLOW | John Earl Jelks |
| AUNT ESTER | Phylicia Rashad |
| BLACK MARY | Yvette Ganier |
| RUTHERFORD SELIG | Raynor Scheine |
| SOLLY TWO KINGS | Anthony Chisholm |
| CAESAR | Peter Francis James |

The play was produced on September 24, 2004, at Huntington Theatre Company (Nicholas Martin, Artistic Director; Michael Maso, Managing Director) in Boston. It was presented by special arrangement with Sageworks. The director was Kenny Leon and the consulting producer was Benjamin Mordecai; the set design was by David Gallo, the costume design was by Constanza Romero, the lighting design was by Donald Holder, the sound design was by Dan Moses Schreier, the original music was composed and arranged by Kathryn Bostic; the fight director was J. Allen Suddeth, the dramaturg was Todd Kreidler, the production stage manager was Narda E. Alcorn and the stage manager was Jason Rossman. The cast was as follows:

| | |
|---|---|
| ELI | Eugene Lee |
| CITIZEN BARLOW | John Earl Jelks |
| AUNT ESTER | Phylicia Rashad |
| BLACK MARY | LisaGay Hamilton |
| RUTHERFORD SELIG | Raynor Scheine |

| | |
|---|---|
| SOLLY TWO KINGS | Anthony Chisholm |
| CAESAR | Ruben Santiago-Hudson |

On December 6, 2004, this production of *Gem of the Ocean* opened on Broadway at the Walter Kerr Theatre with the same cast and creative team. It was produced by Carole Shorenstein Hays and Jujamcyn Theaters, in association with Robert G. Bartner. The production supervisors were Neil A. Mazzella and Gene O'Donovan.

## CHARACTERS

ELI, Aunt Ester's gatekeeper and longtime friend of Solly.

CITIZEN BARLOW, a young man from Alabama who is in spiritual turmoil. Late twenties/early thirties.

AUNT ESTER TYLER, a very old, yet vital spiritual advisor for the community.

BLACK MARY, Aunt Ester's protégé and housekeeper. Late twenties.

RUTHERFORD SELIG, a traveling peddler who is a frequent visitor of the house.

SOLLY TWO KINGS, suitor to Aunt Ester, former Underground Railroad conductor. Sixty-seven.

CAESAR WILKS, Black Mary's brother and local constable. About fifty-two.

## SETTING

The play is set in 1904, the Hill District, Pittsburgh, Pennsylvania, in the parlor of Eli, Aunt Ester and Black Mary's home at 1839 Wylie Avenue.

# PROLOGUE

*The lights come up on Eli in the kitchen. It is late night. He is preparing to retire. He draws the shade and is preparing to put out the light when there is a knock at the door. The knock grows insistent. Eli finally goes and answers the door. Citizen Barlow enters. He is agitated.*

ELI: This a peaceful house.

CITIZEN: I come to see Aunt Ester.

ELI: You got to come back Tuesday. She don't see nobody till Tuesday.

CITIZEN: What you mean come back? The people say go see Aunt Ester. This 1839 Wylie ain't it?

ELI: Come back Tuesday.

*(Eli starts to close the door. Citizen pushes his way in.)*

CITIZEN: I ain't going nowhere till I see Aunt Ester.

ELI: You got to come back Tuesday.

(*Citizen tries to go around Eli, who grabs him and shoves him toward the door. They knock over a lamp and Citizen's hat falls off as Eli tussles with him. Aunt Ester enters from her room. Her presence has an immediate calming effect on Citizen. Aunt Ester picks up Citizen's hat, brushes it off, and hands it to him.*)

AUNT ESTER: Didn't he say Tuesday, baby? Go on I'll see you on Tuesday.

(*Citizen takes his hat and goes out the door. Aunt Ester turns around and goes back into her room. The lights go down on the scene.*)

# ACT ONE

## SCENE 1

*The lights come up on Eli and Black Mary in the kitchen. They have just finished breakfast. Eli stands at the window looking out.*

ELI: He still standing there. He been standing there since he left out of here yesterday. Aunt Ester told him she'd see him on Tuesday and he went and stood across the street there. I don't know what he want to see her about. He went right out there and stood across the street. If he go somewhere he come right back. He been out there every time I look.

BLACK MARY: Who is he?

ELI: He didn't say. He just say he wanted to see Aunt Ester. He look like he just come up here. He still wearing clod-hoppers.

BLACK MARY: If he been standing over there he must not have nowhere to go.

ELI: He can go somewhere and sit down. Today's Saturday. Tuesday's a long way to go. Unless he gonna sleep standing up.

BLACK MARY: He waiting to see if Aunt Ester come out.

ELI: He gonna have a long wait. I ain't know her to leave the house in the past twenty years.

BLACK MARY: He probably go down under the Brady Street Bridge to sleep. They got a whole bunch of people sleeping down there.

ELI: They gonna have some more the way Caesar keep evicting people. He put out two more families yesterday. He charging by the week. They get one week behind and he put them out. He don't ask no questions. He just gather up what little bit of stuff they got and sit it out on the street. Then he arrest them for being out there. What Aunt Ester say?

BLACK MARY: She say no. I asked her if she wanted to get up she say no. I asked her if she was sick she say no.

ELI: It's going on four days now. I ain't never know her to sleep that long. Long as I known her.

BLACK MARY: I asked her did she want anything to eat she say no.

*(There is a knock on the door. Eli goes to answer it. Rutherford Selig enters. He is carrying a frying pan and a can of kerosene.)*

ELI: Hey Selig, come on in.

SELIG: Hey Eli. Here's your kerosene. I got your rocks on the wagon. Say Black Mary I got you that frying pan.

*(Black Mary takes the frying pan and looks at it.)*

That's good iron. You can't get iron like that every day. That's high-grade iron. The bottom's nice and flat.

BLACK MARY: How much you gonna charge me? I paid too much for that coffeepot.

SELIG: I'll let you have it for two dollars. That's a three-dollar frying pan. For you it's two dollars. I would charge you fifty cents more but that's my last one like that and I'll be glad to get rid of it . . . get me a new order. You want the fourteen-inch? I'll have that next week.

BLACK MARY: I paid too much for that coffeepot. I don't want to pay too much for this frying pan.

SELIG: Well, how about dustpans? I'll let you have a dustpan with it for two dollars and twenty-five cents.

*(Black Mary hesitates.)*

I'll tell you what. Make it the two dollars and I'll just give you the dustpan.

*(Black Mary gives him two dollars.)*

Say Eli, I come from upriver. I see where they got the mill shut down.

ELI: They had a man named Garret Brown who jumped into the river. Caesar chased him and he jumped in and wouldn't come out. They say he stole a bucket of nails. He said he didn't do it. They having his funeral today.

SELIG: I seen the people standing around down at the church. They got a bunch of people standing around down there. I was wondering what they standing around there for.

ELI: They gonna bury him this afternoon. They gonna bury him out of Reverend Tolliver's church. They was supposed to bury him yesterday out of Reverend Flowers' church but Caesar stopped them. He went up to Reverend Flowers and told him it was against the law. The Christian law. Man ain't set foot in a church for thirty years talking about the Christian law. Caesar's just mad at him 'cause he didn't get a chance at him.

BLACK MARY: He could have come out of the water.

ELI: They couldn't get him to come out. Caesar told him he wasn't gonna arrest him. Told him he'd give him a bowl of soup and some dry clothes. He told Caesar to go to hell. Told his whole family to go to hell. He talking about you, Black Mary.

SELIG: You can't stay in there but so long. That cold will get to you and shut your body down.

ELI: He just treading water. Holding on to the barge. Caesar see he wasn't gonna come out he tried to beat him over the head with a two-by-four. Talking about he wasn't gonna do nothing to him. I believe he would have killed him right on the spot if he came out.

BLACK MARY: He wouldn't have done nothing but arrest him and the judge give him thirty days.

ELI: Well, as it is he dead.

SELIG: If he jumped in the river and didn't come out I'd have to believe he didn't do it. They had a man down in Kentucky was accused of stealing a horse. He said he didn't do it. Turned him into an outlaw. Made him the biggest horse thief in Kentucky. He lived to steal horses. He must of stole five hundred horses. And every one he sent back word: I stole that one but I didn't steal the first one. I stole that one but I didn't steal the first one. They never did catch him. He died and the horse thieving stopped. My daddy told me about it.

*(There is a knock on the door. Eli goes to answer it. Solly enters singing "I Belong to the Band." He is sixty-seven years old. He wears a long coat and a battered hat. He carries a basket and a stick.)*

SOLLY *(Singing)*:
    I belong to the band
    I belong to the band
    I belong to the band, oh yes I do
    Talking about that Railroad Band.

ELI: Hey Solly, come on in.

SOLLY: The people say they ain't going back to work at the mill. They lining up for the funeral down at the church. They lining up all around the block. Look like every Negro in Pittsburgh down there.

ELI: Reverend Tolliver's gonna get rich. The people appreciate him opening up his church.

BLACK MARY: Why don't you leave that basket outside? I told you leave it out there.

SOLLY: I'm afraid somebody's gonna run off with it.

BLACK MARY: Who's gonna steal a basket of dog shit?

SOLLY: It's pure! It's called pure! They got pure collectors all over the world. People been collecting pure for four hundred years.

BLACK MARY: I don't care what it's called. Who would want to steal it.

SOLLY: Anybody would steal it. Look here. (*Pulls some money out of his pocket*) Where you think this come from? It come from this basket of pure. People will kill people over money. You know if they kill somebody over money they will steal anything that ain't nailed down.

BLACK MARY: Talking about somebody stealing a basket of dog shit.

SOLLY: A lot of people get confused by this pure. They don't know the shoemakers use it to work the leather. I had one old gal tell me, "Get on away from me you smell like dog shit." I showed her that two dollars I got from Butera and she told me come and go home with her. Cooked me up a whole pan of cornbread. I went on back up there and she was gone. I don't know what happened to her.

SELIG: There is a lot of them like that. Where you don't know what happened with them.

SOLLY: I do have my Special Rider though. She up on Webster. I'd marry her if I wasn't in love with somebody else.

BLACK MARY: Here, Selig. I baked you a loaf of bread.

SELIG: I thank you Black Mary. That way I won't have to stop by Caesar's bakery. I got to get on. I'll unload them rocks out back.

*(Selig gets up to leave. Eli hands him two dollars.)*

ELI: Thanks, Selig.

SELIG: If you need any more rocks you let me know. I can get you some cobblestones if you want.

ELI: Naw, I like the rocks.

SOLLY: Hey Selig. I see you got a new horse.

SELIG: Ain't she a beauty? Name's Sally. I got her from Jacob Herlich. He going up to New York to go in business with his brother.

SOLLY: Yeah, that's a nice-looking horse.

SELIG: I ain't had a speck of trouble out of her since I had her. I say get up and she go. Whoa and she stop. I feed her some oats and she carry me wherever I want to go. If everything go right I'm gonna get me a new wagon. See you next time, Black Mary. Tell Aunt Ester I asked about her.

BLACK MARY: Take care of yourself, Selig.

*(Selig exits. Eli crosses back over to the window.)*

ELI: Come on and help me build this wall.

SOLLY: Where you building a wall at?

ELI: Out back. I'm gonna take and build a wall around the side there.

SOLLY: You can get you some wood and build you a fence.

ELI: I want a wall.

SOLLY: I'll help you. When you wanna start?

ELI: Anytime you ready. We can start tomorrow.

SOLLY: All right.

ELI: I want a wall. See if I can keep Caesar on the other side. The way he going he gonna have everybody in jail.

BLACK MARY: Caesar's doing his job. That's what the people can't see.

SOLLY: Caesar's the kind of people I would want working for me. If I ever get me a plantation I'm gonna hire him to keep my niggers in line.

I got a letter from my sister. Hey, Black Mary . . . read this for me. (Hands her the letter)

BLACK MARY (Reads):

Dear Solomon,

I am writing to let you know the times are terrible here the most anybody remember since bondage. The people are having a hard time with freedom. I can't hold on here anymore. The white peoples is gone crazy and won't let anybody leave. They beat one fellow on the road so bad his mama say, "Who is he?" They killed some more and say the colored can't buy any tickets on the train to get away. Say they will sink the ferry if any colored on it. I want to leave to come North but it is too bad. It is a hard time for everybody. Write and let me know what to do as I try to hold on but can't.

Your loving sister,
Eliza Jackson

SOLLY: I got to go back down there.

ELI: I would go with you but I got to take care of Aunt Ester.

SOLLY: I got to go back down there and get my sister. I'm gonna see if Jefferson Culpepper wanna go with me.

ELI: I'm surprised Jefferson Culpepper can walk old as he is. You talking about eight hundred miles. Eight hundred miles one way is eight hundred miles coming back. He need to go find him a rocking chair somewhere.

SOLLY: I believe I can make it back down there if I don't get sleepy. I get sleepy sometime and don't know if I got it mixed up with the time and it really be night even though it look like the daytime. A lot of things can fool you like that. A lot of things shine like gold ain't gold. A lot of brass shine like gold.

(*Aunt Ester enters.*)

AUNT ESTER: What you doing making all that noise out here? I smell pigfeet. Black Mary, put me on a pot of tea. Eli, see if you can get that stove in there to work. I don't know what it is. Seem like I be cold all the time.

ELI: You ain't getting sick is you?

AUNT ESTER: I ain't said I was sick I'm just cold. I don't know what it is.

(*Eli exits into Aunt Ester's room.*)

SOLLY: I brought you some pure.

AUNT ESTER: Black Mary, see what he got there.

SOLLY: I got a little bit of everything. Got some thirty-day. Got some sixty-day.

AUNT ESTER: See what it look like, Black Mary.

(*Black Mary takes one of the bags and opens it and looks inside.*)

You can't tell nothing by looking at it. Bring it here! How you gonna be scared of dog shit? That's all it is.

BLACK MARY: I ain't said I was scared of it.

AUNT ESTER: Bring it here!

(*Black Mary takes her the bag. Aunt Ester breaks open a piece of pure and empties it in her hand.*)

Look at that. God made that! Ain't nothing in God's creation that ain't good. Look at that. See he ain't been eating nothing but bone. Give me some of this, Solly. What else you got?

(*Black Mary exits up the stairs.*)

SOLLY: There's a Great Dane up on Arcena Street. I been trying to get some of that but he don't never let him out. Great big old dog. Look like a small horse.

AUNT ESTER: They say that helps with tomatoes. But I'll be satisfied with this.

(*She takes some coins out of a small purse and gives them to Solly.*)

I don't know what got in that child. Seem like she don't want to learn nothing.

SOLLY: Black Mary stubborn. Her and Caesar just alike. Only she ain't got his evilness. But she got everything else. They say the apple don't fall too far from the tree. But sometime it fall far enough. That's the difference between her and Caesar. The apple fell and then it rolled a little bit.

(*Black Mary enters carrying her purse.*)

BLACK MARY: I'm going shopping.

AUNT ESTER: I thought you was gonna do the laundry.

BLACK MARY: I got to go down on Logan Street.

AUNT ESTER: It ain't like it's gonna do itself. You got to plan better. I told you the key is to plan. You plan right you can unlock any door. You got to run down on Logan Street *and* do the laundry. You got to do both.

BLACK MARY: I ain't say I wasn't gonna do it. I said I'm going out now.

*(Black Mary exits.)*

AUNT ESTER: She running down there to see Percy Saunders. I know where she going. She used to go see Percy Saunders and Robert Smiley. I done told her the people gonna throw stones at her.

SOLLY: You can't keep a man and a woman apart. They was made for each other. That's what I'm trying to tell you. Every time I see you it make me feel good.

AUNT ESTER: You tell that to all the women. They say you got one on every street. You must not have none on Wylie Avenue.

SOLLY: I got two! One for each arm. Everybody know that. But what they don't know is I don't want that no more. You the only one know that. You the only one need to know. I been blessed. You know how they say count your blessings? I can't count that far. I never did live my life for a woman. That's one blessing I ain't had. I'm never in one place long enough. If I lived life for a woman I couldn't live it for the people. The Bible say you can't serve two masters.

AUNT ESTER: Come on and let's get married. You always talking about getting married. I done had four husbands I might as well have five. I'm trying to catch up with Black Mary. She told me she had seventeen husbands.

SOLLY: Black Mary ain't had no husbands. She too stubborn.

AUNT ESTER: She had seventeen rings and I give her a dime for each one of them. That was in a dream I had about Black Mary before I known her. I had that dream and the next day Black Mary knocked on the door and asked me if I had any laundry that needed washing. I told her to go upstairs and make up that bed 'cause anybody willing to do laundry was welcome to stay here. That's three years ago. She been here ever since. I had a dream about you last night.

SOLLY: My dreams won't stay in one place long enough for me to remember them.

AUNT ESTER: I dreamed you had a ship full of men and you was coming across the water. Had that stick and you was standing up in this boat full of men. You come and asked me what I was doing standing there. I told you I wanted to go back across the ocean. I asked you to take me. You said you had some work to do but that you would come back. Told me you had a magic stick and when you come back you would part the water so I could walk across. You come on back and all your men had drowned and the boat was sinking. You said you was going to get another boat and some more men. Said you would come back and smote the water. Then you walked off with that stick. Said you was going to Alabama.

SOLLY: I just got a letter from my sister today. I got to go! She say she can't hold on no more. Say the white people have gone crazy. I got to go back down there to get her. Eli say he staying here with you. But I got to go get my sister. This my last trip. I'm getting old. I can't do more than one more. I don't know what I'm gonna do then. I was thinking about living my life for you. But I got to go back down there and get my sister.

*(Eli enters from Aunt Ester's room.)*

ELI: I got that stove working. Just leave it set like it is. If it get too hot in there let me know.

*(Eli goes to the coat rack to get his coat and hat.)*

Solly, you ready to go down to Garret Brown's funeral?

*(Solly goes to get his coat and hat.)*

AUNT ESTER: Come on back and get some of these pigfeet.

SOLLY: I want more than pigfeet. But I don't think you gonna give me none.

AUNT ESTER: Go on you old rascal you!

(*Solly and Eli exit. The lights go down on the scene.*)

## SCENE 2

*The lights come up on the parlor. Citizen Barlow enters from the upstairs window. There is a knock on the door. No one answers. Another knock. Silence. Citizen enters from upstairs. Hungry, he heads straight for the kitchen and finds the bread box. He grabs a piece of bread, stuffs it in his mouth, grabs another piece, stuffs it in his pocket. He looks around for something else to eat when Aunt Ester enters from her room.*

AUNT ESTER: I didn't know that window was still open up there. No wonder I'm cold.

(*Citizen is startled. He doesn't know what to do.*)

CITIZEN: I ain't gonna harm nobody.

AUNT ESTER: Eli gone out. He ain't coming back for a while. Black Mary gone shopping. Are you hungry? She got them pigfeet on but they ain't done yet. She gonna make up a pot of soup when she come back.

CITIZEN: I ain't no robber. You said to come back Tuesday. I can't wait till Tuesday. I can't wait. I have to see you now. They say you can help me. They say you wash people's souls.

AUNT ESTER: God the only one can wash people's souls. God got big forgiveness.

CITIZEN: The people say, "Go see Aunt Ester."

AUNT ESTER: You remind me of my Junebug. He was a nice-looking man like you. Had big hands. Do they call you Junebug? What's your name? My name is Ester Tyler. Some people call me Aunt Ester. What they call you?

CITIZEN: Citizen. They call me Citizen Barlow.

AUNT ESTER: Were you looking for money, Mr. Citizen? I'd give you two dollars if I had my purse. Go in that room and get my purse and I'll give you two dollars. In the room there on the nightstand. You can go and get it and I'll give you two dollars.

CITIZEN: I ain't looking for no money. I ain't no robber. I come to see you.

AUNT ESTER: You remind me of my Junebug he was the only one of my boys that caused me trouble. But I do believe he was a good boy. Just a rascal of a man. Is you a rascal, Mr. Citizen? I believes you is. Come sit down and keep me company. I get lonely sometimes. Do you ever get lonely? Being lonely is hard when there so many people around. I told myself I'm gonna die from loneliness. There was a man who ran and jumped in the river. They say he stole a bucket of nails. Did you hear about that? He died a lonely death. Wasn't nobody but him. All them people standing around watching and he was the only one who died.

CITIZEN: He could have come out the river.

AUNT ESTER: That's the only way he had to say he was innocent. It must have meant an awful lot for him to say that. He was willing to die to say that.

CITIZEN: I was standing there. I seen him. I thought he was gonna come out. I told myself he was gonna come out. The people was telling him to come on out then he just sunk down in the water. He kept saying he didn't steal the bucket of nails. Everything they say to him he just say he didn't steal the bucket of nails.

AUNT ESTER: Jesus Christ was falsely accused. He died a bitter death on the cross. This man was like Jesus. He say he would rather die innocent than to live guilty. You can go ahead and eat your bread, Mr. Citizen. Black Mary be back in a minute. I'll have her make up a pot of soup and some cornbread. You like cornbread? You look like you can eat a whole pan yourself.

CITIZEN: I like cornbread. Yeah.

AUNT ESTER: What you like best cornbread or biscuits? I can never make up my mind.

CITIZEN: I like cornbread but I like biscuits better.

AUNT ESTER: That was like my Junebug. I lost my Junebug, Mr. Citizen. Oh that was a sad time. The darkest day I ever did see was the day I lost my Junebug. You ever looked at a piece of rope, Mr. Citizen? God made that rope. It come right out the ground. You twist and weave it all together and you get a rope. Rope can help you do a lot of things. You tie it around a bucket and you can get water out of a well. You can tie things together with a piece of rope. God made the rope. It's man who sometimes gets in the way of God's creation and turns it over to the devil. Did you ever have love, Mr. Citizen? I've seen people have love and didn't know it. I had love and didn't know it. It's like money you can't ever have enough. You ever had enough money, Mr. Citizen? Some people ain't never had enough.

CITIZEN: I ain't got no money, Miss Tyler. I ain't never had none. Time I get it seem like it belong to somebody else. I owe the mill a lot of money.

AUNT ESTER: Where was you born, Mr. Citizen?

CITIZEN: Alabama. I only been up here four weeks. When I left Alabama they had all the roads closed to the colored people. I had to sneak out. Say they didn't want anybody to leave. Say we had to stay there and work. I told my mama I was going and she say okay. Told me, "There a big world out there." I kissed her. She told me she loved me and I left. I almost got caught a couple of times. I had to go out the back way and find my own roads. Took me almost two weeks. There was some other people out on the road and we helped each other. Me and a fellow named Roper Lee went over to the mill. They say they was paying two dollars a day but when we got there they say a dollar fifty. Then they say we got to pay two dollars room and board. They sent us over to a place the man say we got to put two dollars on top of that. Then he put two men to a room with one bed. The fellow I was with want to fight about it. I'm just starting out I don't want no trouble. I told him I would sleep on the floor. I wasn't planning on sleeping there long. I'm just starting out sleeping there. I asked one fellow what board meant. He say they supposed to give you something to eat. They ain't give us nothing. I say okay. I can't make them give me nothing. What I'm gonna do? I got to eat. I bought a loaf of bread for a dime. A bowl of soup cost ten cents around the corner. I wasn't desperate. I had sixty-five cents to make it to payday. I ate half the bread and say I would get a bowl of soup tomorrow. Come payday they give me three dollars say the rest go on my bill. I had to give the man what own the house two dollars. What I'm gonna do, Miss Tyler? I told the people at the mill I was gonna get another job. They said I couldn't do that 'cause I still owed them money and they was gonna get the police on me. I was gonna go to another city but then before I had a chance I killed a man. I don't know, Miss Tyler. I feel like I got a hole inside me. People say you can help me. I don't want to go to hell, Miss Tyler. My mama cry every time something bad happen to me.

AUNT ESTER: It all will come to stand in the light, Mr. Citizen. Everything and everybody got to stand in the light. Jesus Christ stood in the light. The people saw him standing there and they killed him. But the Judgment ain't with the people. The Judgment with God. He the Big

Master. God don't never lie. The people liable to do any-thing. They lie and cheat. That's why God didn't leave the Judgment with the people. Say, "I am the beginning and the end." The people can't say that. They know they gonna come to an earthy grave. The end is already writ for them.

(*Citizen has fallen asleep in the chair. Aunt Ester begins to sing a lullaby:*)

Go to sleep, my child
You don't know the world yet
Go to sleep, my child
The world is not easy
Go to sleep, my child
I am here watching over you
The world is not easy.

(*Black Mary enters from the street carrying groceries. Aunt Ester puts her finger to her lips.*)

Ssshhh . . . Go upstairs and make up that bed in the spare bedroom. Mr. Citizen is gonna stay and help Eli with that wall.

(*Black Mary exits upstairs.*)

You on an adventure, Mr. Citizen. I bet you didn't know that. It's all adventure. You signed up for it and didn't even know it.

(*The lights go down on the scene.*)

## Scene 3

*The lights come up on Eli and Black Mary in the kitchen.*

ELI: I still don't know how he got in the house. I ain't known Aunt Ester to answer a door in twenty-five years.

BLACK MARY: He ain't said too much. I fixed that bed up and he ain't said too much.

ELI: I believe he come in through that hall window up there. Knocked some of that paint off the window. I don't know why she want him to stay in the house. I put him to work on that wall. He out there now busting up them rocks. You got to keep your eye on him.

*(There is a knock on the door. Eli goes to answer it. Solly enters.)*

Hey Solly, come on in.

SOLLY: They had a riot over at the mill. The people said they wasn't going to work and the police tried to make them. They threw bottles at the police and started busting out the windows. The police charged the crowd arresting everybody they could get their hands on. They couldn't arrest them fast enough. The horses trampling the people. Ran right over the top of one fellow. He liable to be crippled for life. They having another meeting down at the church tonight. They say they ain't going to work tomorrow either. Reverend Tolliver told them not to go. Told them the hand of justice was at the gate but the people still had to open it.

*(Solly hands Black Mary the newspaper.)*

Here, Black Mary, read this.

BLACK MARY *(Reads)*: "Garret Brown of Louisville, Kentucky, departed this life September 30, 1904, at Pittsburgh,

Pennsylvania, at midday, in the midst of a life of usefulness and in the fullness of his powers. He was born of slave parents June the 29th 1862, in Charleston, South Carolina. At an early period in his life, interested parties hurried the mother and three children northward, without the protection of a husband and father, to begin a long siege of poverty. Mr. Brown leaves to mourn his unfinished life, a wife and four children, and a host of family and friends."

*(There is a long silence. Then life continues.)*

ELI: I got somebody to help us with that wall. He out there now busting up them rocks. Aunt Ester say he supposed to stay here till the wall is built.

SOLLY: Hey Black Mary, I need you to help me write a letter to my sister.

ELI: What Jefferson Culpepper say?

*(Black Mary gets a pen and paper.)*

SOLLY: Jefferson Culpepper got the consumption. His doctor say he can't go. It don't look like he got much time left.

ELI: You know I'd go with you if I didn't have to stay and take care of Aunt Ester. It'd be like old times.

SOLLY: I'm going if I have to go by myself.

BLACK MARY: What you want the letter to say?

SOLLY: "Dear Eliza, it is a hard time here for everybody too. Hold on the best you can till I get there . . ." You got that?

BLACK MARY: You want to tell her when you coming?

SOLLY: "I promise the fall will not pass before you see me . . . Pretend to go along with everything as it is." Tell her . . . "The best faith is in yourself even though God do have a hand in it." That's all.

BLACK MARY: How you want to sign it?

SOLLY: "Your brother, Two Kings."

*(Aunt Ester enters and goes and sits in her chair.)*

AUNT ESTER: I thought that was you out here. Where's Mr.
　　Citizen?

ELI: He out back. I got him working on that wall.

AUNT ESTER: See if he want something to eat.

*(Eli exits out back.)*

　　Black Mary, you got something for Mr. Citizen to eat?
　　When you leaving, Solly?

SOLLY: I went down to see Butera and got me some new boots.
　　Jefferson Culpepper can't go. He got the consumption.
　　Soon as I break in these boots I got to go.

*(Eli and Citizen enter. Citizen and Black Mary stare at each
other.)*

AUNT ESTER: Good morning, Mr. Citizen. Did you sleep all
　　right?

CITIZEN: I slept good. Yeah.

AUNT ESTER: I want you to meet somebody. That there is
　　Solly. That's Citizen Barlow. Mr. Citizen remind me of
　　my Junebug.

*(Aunt Ester and Black Mary exit out back.)*

SOLLY: My name is Two Kings. Used to be Uncle Alfred.
　　The government looking for me for being a runaway so
　　I changed it.

CITIZEN: My mama named me Citizen after freedom came.
　　She wouldn't like it if I changed my name.

SOLLY: Your mama's trying to tell you something. She put a
　　heavy load on you. It's hard to be a citizen. You gonna have
　　to fight to get that. And time you get it you be surprised

how heavy it is. I used to be called Uncle Alfred back in slavery. I ran into one fellow called me Uncle Alfred. I told him say, "Uncle Alfred dead." He say, "I'm looking at you." I told him, "You looking at Two Kings. That's David and Solomon." He must have had something in his ear 'cause all he heard is Solomon. He say, "I'm gonna call you Solly." The people been calling me Solly ever since. But my name is Two Kings. Some people call me Solomon and some people call me David. I answer to either one. I don't know which one God gonna call me. If he call me Uncle Alfred then we got a big fight.

CITIZEN: You got that stick. My daddy used to carry a stick like that. My daddy carried a stick everywhere he went. If you see my daddy he'd have his stick.

SOLLY: Lots of people carry sticks. Ain't you never heard that "sticks and stones can break my bones but names can never hurt me." This a bone breaker. I tried carrying stones but they was too heavy. I seen a hundred men carry sticks. My daddy carried a stick. He had to fight to carry it. I don't know if them hundred men had to fight but they was carrying them just the same. Why don't you carry one?

CITIZEN: I got my knife.

SOLLY: I got a knife too. Knives is for killing. I thank God I ain't never had to kill nobody. I come close a couple of times. This old gal took a liking to me and her man come after me one time. That's as close as I ever come to killing somebody. I busted him up pretty bad with my stick and she asked me to stop 'cause he was paying her rent and she needed that. Get you a stick and it'll save you a lot of trouble. Where you from?

CITIZEN: Alabama. Down around Opelika.

SOLLY: I'm from Alabama too. They got some good people down there. I been to Opelika. I been all over. I been clear down to the Gulf of Mexico. All through Louisiana and up into Canada. I first set foot in Canada in 1857. I'm going down to Alabama to get my sister. You ought to come and go to Alabama with me. I need a strong man like you. Get you one of these bone breakers and let's go down there and help the people get away.

CITIZEN: I just left. If I go back with you I'll just have to turn around and come back. I'm up here looking for a job. Ain't no jobs down there.

SOLLY: The people think they in freedom. That's all my daddy talked about. He died and never did have it. I say I got it but what is it? I'm still trying to find out. It ain't never been nothing but trouble.

ELI: Freedom is what you make it.

SOLLY: That's what I'm saying. You got to fight to make it mean something. All it mean is you got a long row to hoe and ain't got no plow. Ain't got no seed. Ain't got no mule. What good is freedom if you can't do nothing with it? I seen many a man die for freedom but he didn't know what he was getting. If he had known he might have thought twice about it.

*(Black Mary enters.)*

BLACK MARY: You want a bowl of beans, Solly?

SOLLY: What kind is they? I had a couple of old gals try and poison me. With this one gal the doctor told me I was lucky. Say if I had eaten another bite I would have died. Good thing she couldn't cook. I was just eating to be polite.

BLACK MARY: They baby lima beans cooked up with some ham hocks.

SOLLY: I can't eat no lima beans. They belly busters. But I can eat baby lima beans. They agree with me a little better.

*(Black Mary sets a bowl of lima beans in front of Solly.)*

ELI: When I was a boy we used to say a little rhyme.

> Beans beans the musical fruit
> The more you eat the more you toot
> The more you toot the better you feel
> So have those beans at every meal.

SOLLY: Them big lima beans tell the truth about that. Hey Black Mary, I got another pair of pants and a shirt that needs washing. I ain't got but a dime.

BLACK MARY: Where's all these dollars you be getting from selling that dog shit. Come in here the other day bragging about it.

SOLLY: I'll give you fifteen cents. I just bought a new pair of shoes.

*(Black Mary sets a bowl of lima beans and cornbread in front of Citizen.)*

If I had the fifteen cents I'd give it to you. I try to do the right thing. I always wanna be on the right side. But sometimes I don't know what side that is. They say, "God have planned but the devil have planned also."

BLACK MARY: God ain't never wrong.

SOLLY: God say different things. Say, "I will smite my enemies." Then he tell you to "turn the other cheek." That don't get you nothing but two broke jaws.

BLACK MARY: You wanna be like God. Everything that's for him ain't for you. That's why God threw Lucifer out of heaven.

SOLLY: That's what I'm saying. Lucifer was God's enemy. God ain't turned the other cheek. He picked Lucifer up and threw him down into hell.

BLACK MARY: The Bible say, "Do unto others as you would have them do unto you."

SOLLY: God ain't done that! He didn't want Lucifer to throw *him* out of heaven. He wanted Lucifer to bow down and pledge obedience. That's what he would have Lucifer do unto him. He wasn't gonna bow down and pledge obedience to Lucifer.

(*There is a knock on the door. Eli goes to answer it. Caesar Wilks enters. About fifty-two years old, he is the local constable and Black Mary's brother.*)

ELI: This a peaceful house.
CAESAR: These niggers gone crazy!

(*Caesar takes off his hat and hangs it up and goes and sits at the table.*)

They was over at the mill rioting. Busting out the goddamn windows. Talking about they ain't going to work. They had all kinds of chaos and confusion over there. Police had to arrest about two hundred people. I ain't never seen nothing like it. Want to bust out the goddamn windows! Running around like a pack of animals. Talking about they ain't going to work. You can't have that. The mill losing money. That's three days in a row they ain't went to work. They after me downtown to put a stop to it. I'll give them one more day. They don't go to work tomorrow there gonna be hell to pay.

(*Black Mary sets a bowl of beans in front of Caesar. Caesar notices Citizen.*)

There's another one come to get his soul washed. If I didn't know any better I'd think Aunt Ester was selling moonshine.
ELI: Citizen Barlow is helping me build a wall out back.

CAESAR: What you building a wall for? You don't need a wall. Somebody wanna come in they just climb over. That ain't nothing but a waste of time. You don't have to worry about a honest man. A thief ain't gonna let a wall stop him. He gonna climb over and keep climbing over until he find out crime don't pay. That's the way you stop a thief. A wall ain't gonna do nothing but make him mad. Hey, where you from?

CITIZEN: Alabama.

CAESAR: I don't want to catch you stealing nothing. I catch you stealing something I'm gonna put you in jail. How long you been up here?

CITIZEN: Four weeks.

CAESAR: Get you some shoes. This the city. You don't need them farming boots up here. Get you some shoes and stay out the saloons. You working? Where you working at?

CITIZEN: I'm looking for a job.

CAESAR: Go over to the mill. They got jobs over there. Go over to the mill and tell them I sent you. Either that or go to Philadelphia. They got jobs in Philadelphia. It's too crowded here. Too many niggers breed trouble. Move on down to Philadelphia. If you stay around here you stay out of trouble. My name's Caesar. I'm the boss man around here. What's your name?

CITIZEN: Citizen Barlow.

CAESAR: Are you a troublemaker, Citizen Barlow? You ever been in jail?

CITIZEN: I ain't never been in jail.

CAESAR: That's where you heading. You got to have visible means of support around here. If I see you standing around looking to steal something and you ain't got two dollars in your pocket you going to jail. You understand? Get you a job and stay out of trouble. Stay off the streets.

CITIZEN: I ain't looking to steal nothing.

CAESAR: That's my sister. Black Mary's my sister. I want you to stay away from her. I don't want you looking at her wrong.

BLACK MARY: Leave him alone, Caesar.

CAESAR: I'm just schooling him. I like him. I don't want to see him get in any trouble.

CITIZEN: My mama told me to stay out of trouble.

CAESAR: Your mama told you right. Where you living? You got a place to stay? You got money to pay your rent?

CITIZEN: I ain't got no place.

CAESAR: Come see me. I'll give you a place to stay. You got to pay the rent though. If you can't pay the rent you got to move on let somebody else pay it. You know how to read? You know how to count money?

CITIZEN: I know how to count money good.

CAESAR: Here . . . here go a quarter. I'm gonna see what you do with that. These niggers take and throw their money away in the saloon and get mad when it's gone. I give one fellow a quarter and he turn around and give it to the candy man. I say he could have did something with that quarter. It wasn't much but it was twenty-five cents more than he had. He took and threw it away. He can't see past his nose. He can't see it's all set up for him to do anything he want. See, he could have took and bought him a can of shoe polish and got him a rag. If he could see that far he'd look up and find twenty-five dollars in his pocket. Twenty-five dollars buys you an opportunity. You don't need but five dollars to get in the crap game. That's five opportunities he done threw away. The candy man gonna get him a bigger wagon and another five pound of sugar. He gonna be digging a ditch the rest of his life. I'm gonna see what you do. You turn that twenty-five cents into five dollars and you come and see me and I'll give you a job.

*(Citizen shoves the quarter back across the table.)*

CITIZEN: I don't want nobody to give me nothing.

CAESAR: I can see you one of them hardheaded niggers. You have to bust you upside the head a couple of times. Then you straighten up. You watch yourself. See, 'cause you just got on my list. I told you I'm the boss man around here. Ask anybody. They'll tell you who Caesar is.

ELI: Best be getting back to work on that wall, Citizen. We got a lot of work to do.

*(Citizen exits.)*

CAESAR: Keep your eye on him. That's one you got to watch. Ain't nothing missing is there? He liable to steal the coffeepot.

BLACK MARY: Caesar, why don't you leave him alone.

CAESAR: I ain't saying nothing bad about him. I like him. He remind me of myself when I was a young man. But if I was you I'd keep my eye on him. I'd feed him in the yard.

*(He notices Solly's shoes.)*

I see you got a new pair of shoes, Solly.

SOLLY: I got a new coat too but I'm scared to wear it. People might think I'm a rich man like you.

CAESAR: Money ain't got nobody's name on it. It's floating out there go on and grab you some. I got a new coat too. I'm gonna wear it tomorrow.

SOLLY: If you wear yours I'll wear mine.

ELI: I hear tell Reverend Tolliver went downtown and tried to talk to the mayor.

CAESAR: What makes him think the mayor's gonna see him? The mayor ain't gonna see him. Wanna bury that damn fool out of his church. I told him not to do it. How he gonna get a Christian burial? Man killed himself. He steal a bucket of nails and then go run and jump in the river and stay there till he die. How he gonna get a Christian burial?

SOLLY: He say he didn't do it.

CAESAR: I'd say I didn't do it too if the law was after me. You arrest somebody for loitering and they'll swear they ain't standing there. That don't mean nothing to me 'cause he say he didn't do it. I had witnesses. Five hundred people standing around watching the man drown. I tried to break it up. Get them to go home. But they wanna stand around and watch a damn fool drown himself in the river. I tried to save him but he ain't had enough sense to save himself. People wanna blame me but I got to keep order. Just like them niggers wanna riot over a bucket of nails. Talking about they ain't going to work. Talking about closing the mill down. They don't understand the mill is what hold everything together. If you close down the mill the city would be in chaos. The city needs that tin. They need that tin in Philadelphia. They need it in Detroit and Cincinnati. Industry is what drive the country. Without industry wouldn't nobody be working. That tin put people to work doing other things. These niggers can't see that. They ought to be glad the mill is there. If it wasn't for the mill these niggers wouldn't have no way to pay their rent. Close down the mill and wait and see what happen then. I'll tell you. A hundred niggers is going to jail for trying to steal something. That's what's gonna happen. A hundred niggers is going to jail for loitering. A hundred niggers is going to jail for disturbing the peace after they get mad and start fighting each other. Five hundred babies is gonna go hungry. You gonna have a hundred new prostitutes. People gonna be living on the streets begging for a dime. And all because some damn fool took it upon himself to steal a bucket of nails and run and jump in the goddamn river. You close down the mill you ain't got nothing. Them niggers can't see that. Want to blame me. You know whose fault it is. I'll tell you whose fault it is. It's Abraham Lincoln's fault. He ain't had no idea what he was doing. He didn't know like

I know. Some of these niggers was better off in slavery. They don't know how to act otherwise. You try and do something nice for niggers and it'll backfire on you every time. You try and give them an opportunity by giving them a job and they take and throw it away. Talking about they ain't going to work.

SOLLY: Eli, I got to go. Tell Aunt Ester I'll see her later.

BLACK MARY: I'll have your laundry ready by Thursday, Solly.

CAESAR: I see you still carrying that stick.

SOLLY: Yeah, I still got it. I'm gonna carry it up the hill to the graveyard.

CAESAR: Well now they got laws against that now. I told you that. This ain't the country. This ain't Alabama. This is Pittsburgh. They got laws against carrying a stick in Pittsburgh. That's a weapon.

SOLLY: This a walking stick! Abraham Lincoln carried a walking stick. General Grant carried a walking stick. You didn't arrest him. Go tell General Grant he can't carry a walking stick!

CAESAR: It's against the law to carry a weapon.

SOLLY: The law can go to hell if you telling me I can't carry a walking stick!

*(Solly exits.)*

CAESAR: There must be five hundred thousand different jobs a man can have. Now you tell me how somebody come to picking dog shit up off the street.

ELI: Let me get on back to that wall.

*(Eli exits.)*

CAESAR: And you got him walking around talking about, "Caesar's sister does my laundry." How that make me look? My sister a washerwoman. Why don't you come back to work for me at the bakery? You sitting up here under Aunt Ester just watching time go by. Aunt Ester ain't got no time. She got both feet in the grave just waiting for the body to follow.

BLACK MARY: You don't know nothing about Aunt Ester. She give me more than most other people. I never been so at peace with myself since I been here. I don't want to hear that. You can say whatever you want but I don't want to hear that.

CAESAR: I told you I can help you. You a young woman.

BLACK MARY: I'm doing just fine. You selling magic bread and overcharging rent. Putting people out in the street. I don't want no part of it.

CAESAR: I give good value for my services. I got clean rooms. Quite naturally if you don't pay the rent somebody else will. I try to tell these niggers this the city. This ain't the country. I can't wait till the crop come in. It's taking them a while but they learning. Yeah, I sell magic bread. Got a big sign say you only have to eat half as much to get twice as full. And I charge one and a half times for it. You don't understand I give the people hope when they ain't got nothing else. They take that loaf of bread and make it last twice as long. They wouldn't do that if they didn't pay one and a half times for it. I'm helping the people.

BLACK MARY: Caesar, I done told you I'm satisfied right where I'm at. I don't want to be part of that.

CAESAR: Now . . . see . . . I remember when you was part of it. You was selling hoecakes with me. You was running the bakery. Why can't it be like old times? I miss having you work with me. I remember when we was working together. It wasn't about Caesar or Black Mary. It was about the Wilks family.

BLACK MARY: That was before you killed that boy.

CAESAR: He was a thief! He was stealing. That's about the worse thing you can do. To steal the fruits of somebody else's labor. Go out and work for it! That's what I did. I ain't never stole nothing in my life. That's against the law. Stealing is against the law. Everybody know that.

BLACK MARY: It was a loaf of bread, Caesar. He was stealing a loaf of bread.

CAESAR: I gave him an opportunity to stop. I told him he was under arrest. He started running! With the loaf of bread under his arm! I had to shoot him. You can't do nothing like that and get away with it.

People don't understand the law is everything. What is it not? People think the law is supposed to serve them. But anybody can see you serve it. There ain't nothing above the law. That's what I try and tell these niggers. Everything come under the law. You got to respect the law. Unless you dead. That's the only way you ain't got to respect the law.

BLACK MARY: I remember a time when you would have laughed at him for stealing a loaf of bread. What happened to that, Caesar?

CAESAR: I took an oath to uphold the law. See, you try and be like your mother. I don't know why your mother never liked me. She tried to poison you against me and you let her.

BLACK MARY: See you killing that boy over a loaf of bread ain't got nothing to do with my mother. You always try and hide behind that.

CAESAR: I got to play the hand that was dealt to me. You look around and see you black. You look at the calendar. Slavery's over. I'm a free man. I can get up whatever time I want to in the morning. I can move all over and pick any woman I want. I can walk down the street to the store and buy anything my money will buy. There ain't nothing I can't have. I'm starting out with nothing so I got to get a little something. A little place to start. You look and see the race you got to run is different than somebody else's.

Maybe it's got more hills. It's longer. But this is what I got. Now what to do with it?

I look around and see where niggers got to eat and niggers got to sleep. I say if I had some bread I'd be a rich man. I got some bread. In the valley of the blind the one-eyed man is king. I started selling hoecakes off the back of a wagon. I'd cook them over the coals. I got me some beans. Selling them right out the pot. I even put a little pork in them. Police ran me off the corner. Say I needed a license. It took me a while but I got me a license. I had to pay six or seven people but I got me a license.

Niggers say my bowls was too small. I got bigger bowls. Say I didn't put enough pork in the beans. I put in more pork. I got me some chickens. I charged extra for the big ones and the people got mad. One man told me the chickens had big feet but they didn't have big wings. I seen I was in the wrong business. Said I was gonna let niggers eat on their own and give them a place to sleep. Only I didn't have no money to buy no property.

Went down to the bank to borrow some money. They told me I needed some collateral. Say you need something to borrow money against. I say all right, I'll get me some collateral. I opened me up a gambling joint in the back of the barbershop. Sold whiskey. The police closed it down. I had to put some bullet holes in a couple of niggers and the police arrested me. Put me on the county farm. I had to bust a couple of niggers upside the head for trying to steal my food. A couple tried to escape. I caught them. That don't do nothing but make it harder on everybody. They out there enjoying their freedom ducking and dodging the law and everybody else on half rations and got to make up their work.

A fellow named John Hanson started a riot. I seen that wasn't gonna be nothing but bad news. I took him on one-to-one. Man-to-man. He busted my eye. That's why

I can't see but so good out my one eye. He busted my eye but I put down the riot. They gave me a year. I did six months when the mayor called me in to see him. Say he wanted to put me in charge of the Third Ward. Told me say you fry the little fish and send the big fish to me. They give me a gun and a badge. I took my badge and gun and went down to the bank and laid it on the counter. Told them I wanted to borrow some money on that. There was a fellow name Harry Bryant had a place on Colwell Street he sold me. They ran him out of town. Charged me three times what it was worth. Took the money and ran. They tried to kill him for selling to a Negro. I say all right I got me a little start. Niggers got mad at me. Said I must have thought I was a white man 'cause I got hold to a little something. They been mad at me ever since. Everybody mad at me. You mad at me.

BLACK MARY: It ain't about being mad at you, Caesar. You're my brother. I respect and honor that. I always have and I always will. But we don't owe each other any more than that.

CAESAR: I ain't got but one sister and I try to do right by her and you push me away. Family is important. I know the value of family. Blood is thicker than water. It's been that way and always will be. You can't even water it down.

Your mother wanna turn blood into vinegar. When Uncle Jack was dying she wouldn't even go see him. Say he was fooling the people being a fake blind man. She was right. But that's her brother! He deserve better than that. You can't sit in Judgment over people. That's God's job. God decide who done right or wrong. Uncle Jack dying and calling for his sister and she wouldn't even go and see him. That's the kind of mother you got. You let her run your life. Got you thinking like her. You thinking wrong and don't even know it. Many a time I tried to make up to her but she wouldn't have it. Called me a scoundrel. But that didn't stop me from paying for her funeral. I paid for the funeral and even shed a few tears. If I had known any prayers I would have said them. Why? 'Cause she family. You give up on family and you ain't got nothing left.

(*Caesar exits. The lights go down on the scene.*)

## Scene 4

*The lights come up on Black Mary and Aunt Ester in the kitchen. Black Mary is washing vegetables in the sink.*

AUNT ESTER: When you gonna comb out your hair? You got pretty hair. I don't know why you trying to hide it. Is you getting along with Mr. Citizen? He ain't no trouble is he?

BLACK MARY: He ain't no trouble. Eli trying to figure out how he got in the house.

AUNT ESTER: He knocked on the door and I let him in.

BLACK MARY: Eli say you ain't answered a door in twenty-five years. Say it look like somebody knocked some of the paint off coming through the hall window.

AUNT ESTER: If he knew what he ask for? I told you that's the problem now. People waste their time asking all the wrong questions. The question ain't how he got in. The question is who left the window open? That's the question. I told you don't waste the water. Put them in a pot and wash them off in the pot. (*Slaps Black Mary's hands*) Don't leave all them stems on there. You got that fire too high. Damp that fire down. Wake me up if Solly come back.

(*Aunt Ester exits into her room. Black Mary chops vegetables at the sink. Citizen enters with a bucket.*)

CITIZEN: Eli sent me for some water.

BLACK MARY: There it is over there.

(*Citizen starts to draw the water.*)

You knocked some of the paint off the sill coming through the window.

(*Citizen is taken aback.*)

CITIZEN: I couldn't wait till Tuesday. I got to get my soul washed real bad. You ever had your soul washed?
BLACK MARY: God's the only one can wash your soul.
CITIZEN: The people sent me to see Aunt Ester. One man say he came to see Aunt Ester and all his problems went away. Say she can help anybody.
BLACK MARY: You got to help yourself. Aunt Ester can help you if you willing to help yourself. She ain't got no magic power.
CITIZEN: The people say, "Go see Aunt Ester and get your soul washed."
BLACK MARY: The people say a lot of things.
CITIZEN: I like your hands. You got pretty hands.
BLACK MARY: I do too much laundry to have pretty hands. They're a woman's hands. That's all you see.
CITIZEN: Eli your man?
BLACK MARY: I ain't got no man.
CITIZEN: You too young a woman not to have a man.
BLACK MARY: You a young man . . . do you have a woman?
CITIZEN: I left my woman down in Alabama. We just couldn't get along. We said good-bye with tears in our eyes. You ever left anybody like that?
BLACK MARY: I left and been left.

(*Citizen picks up the bucket and heads toward the door. He stops.*)

CITIZEN: My room right next to yours . . . maybe you wanna come see me tonight.

BLACK MARY: What I want to see you about, Mr. Citizen?

CITIZEN: I got something for you.

BLACK MARY: What you got for me?

CITIZEN: A woman's got needs. I can fill you up.

BLACK MARY: What you know about a woman's needs.

CITIZEN: I don't know all about a woman . . . but I know a woman needs a man.

*(Citizen moves behind her and puts his arms around her. Black Mary pushes him away and twists her way out of his grasp. She looks at him for a beat, then opens her arms, offering herself to him.)*

BLACK MARY: Here, Mr. Citizen. Here.

*(Citizen embraces her. Black Mary lays her head on his chest.)*

You got a woman in your hands. Now what? What you got? What you gonna do? Time ain't long, Mr. Citizen. A woman ain't but so many times filled up. What you gonna do? What you gonna fill me up with? Love? Happiness? Peace? What you got, Mr. Citizen? I seen it all. You got something new? Fill me up, Mr. Citizen. What you got for me, you got something I ain't seen? Come on. What can I be without you?

*(Citizen steps out of her embrace.)*

CITIZEN: I'm a man. I can't change that. You a woman. A man's gonna have his way with a woman. I got the same as everybody else.

*(Black Mary returns to chopping vegetables.)*

BLACK MARY: Leroy. And John. And Cujoe. And Sam. And
Robert. One after the other they come and they go. You
can't hold on to none of them. They slip right through
your hands. They use you up and you can't hold them.
They all the time taking till it's gone. They ain't tried to
put nothing to it. They ain't got nothing in their hand.
They ain't got nothing to add to it. They too busy taking.
They taking 'cause they need. You can't blame them for
that. They so full of their needs they can't see you. Now
here you come. You don't even know what you need. All
you see is a woman. You can't see nothing else. You can't
think nothing else. That blinds you.

*(Black Mary turns to him. A new thought occurs to her.)*

Okay, Mr. Citizen. I'll come to your room tonight. But the
morning got to come, Mr. Citizen. What you got then?
You tell me tomorrow. You wake up and look at your
hands and see what you got.
CITIZEN: I got me. That's all there is.
BLACK MARY: That ain't never gonna be enough.

*(Citizen picks up the bucket and goes out the door.*
*Black Mary chops vigorously as the lights go down on the*
*scene.)*

## SCENE 5

*The lights come up on Aunt Ester and Black Mary in the parlor. Black
Mary is washing Aunt Ester's feet. Aunt Ester is smoking a pipe.*

AUNT ESTER: You think you supposed to know everything.
Life is a mystery. Don't you know life is a mystery? I see
you still trying to figure it out. It ain't all for you to know.

It's all an adventure. That's all life is. But you got to trust that adventure. I'm on an adventure. I been on one since I was nine years old. That's how old I was when my mama sent me to live with Miss Tyler. Miss Tyler gave me her name. Ester Tyler. I don't tell nobody what I was called before that. The only one know that is my mama. I stayed right on there with her till she died. Miss Tyler passed it on to me. If you ever make up your mind I'm gonna pass it on to you. People say it's too much to carry. But I told myself somebody got to carry it. Miss Ester carried it. Carried it right up till the day she died. I didn't run from it. I picked it up and walked with it. I got a strong memory. I got a long memory. People say you crazy to remember. But I ain't afraid to remember. I try to remember out loud. I keep my memories alive. I feed them. I got to feed them otherwise they'd eat me up. I got memories go way back. I'm carrying them for a lot of folk. All the old-timey folks. I'm carrying their memories and I'm carrying my own. If you don't want it I got to find somebody else. I'm getting old. Going on three hundred years now. That's what Miss Tyler told me. Two hundred eighty-five by my count.

BLACK MARY: I ain't say I didn't want it.

AUNT ESTER: You act like it. Run from it all the time. I told myself Black Mary got to make up her mind. I don't know how much time I got left. Go upstairs and get Mr. Citizen. Tell him I want to see him. You can cut my toenails later.

(*Black Mary exits up the stairs. Aunt Ester lights her pipe. Citizen enters from the stairs.*)

Sit on down there, Mr. Citizen. It's been a good day, Mr. Citizen. Has it been a good day for you? Sometimes the days run into one another and you can't tell one from another. I can look at you and see you a man got good taste. My husband was like that. He was a man of good taste. He dead now. I told myself it couldn't be nothing but bad luck. Sometimes it's hard to tell bad luck from good luck but then again sometimes it's easy. Sometimes you're lucky and you don't even know it. Is you lucky, Mr. Citizen? Some people carry their luck with them and some people got to find it. Sometimes you find bad luck and good luck in the same place. I was lucky when I met Rupert and unlucky when I lost him. Tell me about the man you killed. Tell me what you done, Mr. Citizen.

*(Citizen reaches in his bag and pulls out a fistful of nails.)*

CITIZEN: I stole a bucket of nails. The mill wouldn't pay me so I stole a bucket of nails. They say Garret Brown stole it he ran and jumped in the river. I told myself to tell them I did it but every time I started to tell them something got in the way. I thought he was gonna come out the water but he never did. I looked up and he had drowned. It's like I got a hole inside me. If I ain't careful seem like everything would leak out that hole. What to do, Miss Tyler?

AUNT ESTER: I know a man used to raise pigs. Great big old pigs. To him the pig was the beginning of everything. And it was the end of everything. Wherever he looked he saw pigs. He saw pigs in the sky and he saw pigs in the ground. To him the pig was the center of his life. One day another man come along and killed all his pigs. He lost everything he had. He lost the center of his life 'cause it wasn't inside him. It wasn't something nobody could take away. See, Mr. Citizen, right now that bucket of nails is at the center of your life. You only have one life, Mr. Citizen. It's your life. Can't nobody else claim it. You ain't never gonna for-get that man who jumped in the river. There are times when it will come and take hold of you and shake you. There ain't nothing you can do about that. It's them in-between times that you can do something about. You got to find something else to be at the center of your life. You got to find out why it was important for Garret Brown to die rather than to take his thirty days. Do you know why he didn't come out the water, Mr. Citizen? Do you know why he chose to die rather than to be branded a thief?

CITIZEN: 'Cause he didn't do it.

AUNT ESTER: We know he didn't do it. But why, Mr. Citizen. That's what we trying to find out why he would rather die than to say he was a thief.

CITIZEN: 'Cause everybody would know. When they see him they say, "There go the man who stole the bucket of nails."

AUNT ESTER: He didn't care if anybody else knew if he did it or not. He knew. He didn't do it for the people standing around watching. He did it for himself. He say I'd rather die in truth than to live a lie. That way he can say that his life is worth more than a bucket of nails. What is your life worth, Mr. Citizen? That what you got to find out. You got to find a way to live in truth. If you live right you die right. Like Garret Brown. Do you know the story of Peter from the Bible? Peter denied Jesus three times before the cock crowed. That's what the Bible say. Say, "Verily verily I say unto you before the cock crow you will deny me thrice." They asked Peter, "Do you know this man?" And Peter said, "No, I don't know him." Not once, Mr. Citizen. Three times. He say it one time then he had a chance to think about it before he said it again. Right there he could have redeemed himself. What do you think, Mr. Citizen? Why did he deny him three times? Would you have denied him three times?

CITIZEN: I don't know, Miss Tyler. I don't know much about the Bible.

AUNT ESTER: The Bible say Peter denied Christ three times. I always wondered about that. He had his redemption handed to him on a silver platter but he didn't take it.

I wonder will you take yours, Mr. Citizen. (*Calls*) Black Mary!

If the wheel don't turn the right way you got to fix it. I know a man went to fix the wheel. It was turning backwards instead of forward. He went to fix it and time he was through the wheel didn't turn at all. You got to be careful. Things ain't always what they seem.

(*Black Mary enters.*)

Mr. Citizen, listen to what I tell you. I'm gonna help you. I'm gonna tell you about the City of Bones but first I'm gonna send you upriver. When you get there I want you to look around and find two pennies lying on the ground. They got to be lying side by side. You can't find one on one street and another on another street. They got to be lying side by side. If you see one laying by itself just let it lay there. When you find them two pennies I want you to put them in your handkerchief and bring them straight back to me. Where's your coat and hat? Go get your coat and hat.

(*Citizen exits up the stairs.*)

Black Mary, draw that shade and get me a candle. Where's Eli?

BLACK MARY: He's gone to the meeting at the church.

AUNT ESTER: The people will come and tell you anything. They got all kinds of problems. They tell you this and they tell you that. You'll come to find out most of the time they looking for love. Love will go a long way toward making you right with yourself. They looking for love and don't know what it is. If you tell them they still don't know. You got to show them how to find it for themselves.

(*Citizen enters with his coat and hat.*)

Mr. Citizen, I want you to follow the Monongahela River clear up to Blawnox. There's a man named Jilson Grant. Ask anybody where you can find him. Jilson Grant. Tell him Aunt Ester sent you. You be careful, Mr. Citizen. Don't forget, Jilson Grant. He's gonna give you something. Then you take and put that in your handkerchief with the two pennies and bring it straight back to me. Go on, now.

(*Citizen exits. Aunt Ester lights a vigil candle and goes and sets it in the window.*)

BLACK MARY: What's the two pennies for? Why he got to find two pennies?

AUNT ESTER: That's only to give him something to do. He think there a power in them two pennies. He think when he find them all his trouble will be over. But he need to think that before he can come face to face with himself. Ain't nothing special about the two pennies. Only thing special about them is he think they special. He find them two pennies then he think he done something. But, he ain't done nothing but find two pennies.

(*In the distance they hear the sound of fire bells. Eli, out of breath from running, bursts in the front door.*)

ELI: The mill's on fire! The mill's burning. Great big fire.

(*The lights go down on the scene.*)

# ACT TWO

*The lights come up on Black Mary and Selig in the kitchen the next morning.*

SELIG: That's all anybody talking about. They talking about it clear down in Philadelphia. They say somebody started that fire at the mill. Say the colored is still mad over the man who jumped into the river. They talking about keeping the colored out of Pennsylvania. Say, "What do we need them for?" One man say they ought to send them back down South. I come on past the general store in Rankin and they was talking about, "Why can't we have slavery again?" One man said 'cause of the law. And somebody said change the law. The man asked him, "Would you fight another war?" And he said, "Hell yeah." I was surprised when he said that but then I wasn't too surprised. They talking about bringing in the army if the police can't handle it.

*(Aunt Ester enters from her room.)*

AUNT ESTER: How you doing, Mr. Selig?

SELIG: I'm doing all right, Aunt Ester. Fixing to go back up-river. Everybody's talking about the fire at the mill.

AUNT ESTER: Where is Eli?

BLACK MARY: He gone out to see if he could find out any more news.

AUNT ESTER: It's a hard time for everybody, Mr. Selig. I do believe the spirit is willing but the people can't get their bodies to follow along with it. There's too much trouble. It's always been trouble and it look like it always will be. I ask myself why that is and I can't come up with an answer.

SELIG: My mama say trouble is man-made. Say if man didn't make trouble it wouldn't have to follow you. She say, "Trouble will follow you to your grave."

AUNT ESTER: Black Mary, where's your hospitality? You got a biscuit over there for Mr. Selig? Give Mr. Selig a biscuit. I know he like his biscuits.

*(Black Mary gives Selig a biscuit.)*

SELIG: I thank you, Black Mary.

*(Eli enters the front door. He notices Selig.)*

ELI: It's still burning. They haven't put the fire out yet. Don't look like they can put it out. They say somebody seen who started it.

SELIG: Yeah, that all anybody's talking about. I just come from seeing my girlfriend in Rankin. They talking about it up there. I didn't know somebody seen him. I don't know why somebody would burn down the mill. Where the people gonna work at now? It don't make much sense to me.

ELI: That was the biggest fire I ever seen. They had every fire wagon in Pittsburgh trying to put that fire out. The wind didn't help none. The wind catch the flames and it lit up the whole sky. They had a bunch of fellows got hurt trying to put that fire out.

SELIG: Well let me get on. I unloaded some more rocks out back for you, Eli. I see that wall's coming along.

ELI: Yeah, that boy's a good worker. We be finished in another two, three days. *(Paying Selig)* Thanks.

SELIG: I'm going back upriver tonight. I'm gonna stop down and see my girlfriend in Scotch Bottom and then head on back upriver. Thanks for the biscuit, Black Mary. Aunt Ester, I'm gonna try and stay out of trouble but I don't think it's gonna work.

AUNT ESTER: Go on you old buzzard. Take care of yourself now. You be careful out there.

*(Selig exits. There is a knock on the door. Eli goes to answer it. Citizen enters.)*

CITIZEN: I got the two pennies. Aunt Ester say to come back then.

AUNT ESTER: Come on in, Mr. Citizen.

CITIZEN: I got the two pennies, Miss Tyler.

AUNT ESTER: Come on, Mr. Citizen, and tell me about them pennies.

CITIZEN: They was laying there. Side by side. I picked them up. Somebody must have just lost them 'cause they brand-new. They still shining. I was looking for Jilson Grant. I never did find him. Nobody knew who he was.

AUNT ESTER: Everybody know Jilson Grant. You must not have been in Blawnox. I bet you only got as far as Clairton.

CITIZEN: I walked around till I got tired. It started to rain. I found a bridge and went down under there till it stopped. I was coming up around near the bakery so

I could buy a loaf of bread and I looked and saw them two pennies lying there side by side. They still shining.

(Citizen hands Aunt Ester the two pennies. Aunt Ester goes over and blows out the vigil candle.)

AUNT ESTER: Black Mary, go get the map. I got something I want to show Mr. Citizen.

(Black Mary exits up the stairs.)

Some people don't like adventure, Mr. Citizen. They stay home. Like me. I done seen all the adventure I want to see. I been across the water. I seen both sides of it. I know about the water. The water has its secrets the way the land has its secrets. Some know about the land. Some know about the water. But there is some that know about the land and the water. They got both sides of it. Then you got the fire. That's a special one. It's got lots of secrets. Fire will heal and kill. It's tricky like that. I can talk about the land and I can talk about the fire. But I don't talk about the water. There was a time, Mr. Citizen, when God moved on the water. And sometime he moves on the land. Is he moving now? We don't know. We can't all the time see it.

(Black Mary enters with a quilt on which there is a map.)

Take a look at this map, Mr. Citizen. See that right there . . . that's a city. It's only a half mile by a half mile but that's a city. It's made of bones. Pearly white bones. All the buildings and everything is made of bones. I seen it. I been there, Mr. Citizen. My mother live there. I got an aunt and three uncles live down there in that city made of bones. You want to go there, Mr. Citizen? I can take you there if you want to go. That's the center of the world. In time it will all come to light. The people made a kingdom out of nothing. They were the people that didn't make it across the water. They sat down right there. They say, "Let's make a kingdom. Let's make a city of bones." The people got a burning tongue, Mr. Citizen. Their mouths are on fire with song. That water can't put it out. That song is powerful. It rise up and come across the water. Ten thousand tongues and ten thousand chariots coming across the water. They on their way, Mr. Citizen. They coming across the water. Ten thousand hands and feet coming across the water. They on their way. I came across that ocean, Mr. Citizen. I cried. I had lost everything. Everything I had ever known in this life I lost that. I cried a ocean of tears. Did you ever lose anything like that, Mr. Citizen? Where you so lost the only thing that can guide you is the stars. That's all I had left. Everything I had ever known was gone to me. The only thing I had was the stars. I say well I got something. I wanted to hold on to them so I started naming them. I named them after my children. I say there go Seefus and that's Jasper and that's Cecilia, and that big one over there that's Junebug. You ever look at the stars, Mr. Citizen? I bet you seen my Junebug and didn't even know it. You come by here sometime when the stars are out and I'll show you my Junebug. You come by anytime you want. You got the stars but it's that wind what drive the boat, Mr. Citizen. Without the wind it would just sit there. But who drives the wind? What god drives the wind? That's what I asked myself but I didn't have no answer. So I just started singing. Just singing quietly to myself some song my mother had taught me. After that it was all right for a little while. But the wind did drive the boat right across the water. What it was driving me to I didn't know. That's what made it so hard. And I didn't have my mother to tell me. That made it harder.

*(During the previous Aunt Ester has made a small boat from her document of a Bill of Sale. She shows the boat to Citizen.)*

You see that, Mr. Citizen. That's a boat. You gonna take a ride on that boat.

*(She hands it to him.)*

Do you believe you can take a ride on that old boat, Mr. Citizen?

CITIZEN: This a piece of paper.

AUNT ESTER: That not what you call your ordinary boat. Look at that boat, Mr. Citizen. That's a magic boat. There's a lot of power in that boat. Power is something. It's hard to control but it's hard to stand in the way of it. God sweep the stars aside, Mr. Citizen. He don't let nothing stand in his way. God don't know nothing but the truth. That boat can take you to that city, Mr. Citizen. Do you believe it can take you to that city?

CITIZEN: I don't know, Miss Tyler.

AUNT ESTER: If you believe it can take you. God got room for everybody. I don't know if you ever seen him but God wear all different kinds of clothes. He got all kinds of faces and he got a sword. It's a big sword. The Bible say it's a mean and terrible swift sword. And when he get to waving that sword around he can do anything. I can take you to that city, but you got to want to go. Do you want to go, Mr. Citizen? Do you want to get your soul washed?

CITIZEN: I got to get this thing off me, Miss Tyler. Yeah, I want to go.

AUNT ESTER: Listen to what I tell you. We gonna go to the City of Bones tonight but first you got to get ready. I want you to go and take a bath. Get scrubbed real good. Then I want you to put on your best clothes then go into your room and pray. Even if you don't know how to pray I want you to try. Black Mary, heat up some water for Mr. Citizen and then go get things ready. I'm going to get myself ready. Do not disturb me.

(*The lights go down on the scene.*)

## Scene 2

*The lights come up on Black Mary and Eli in the kitchen.*

BLACK MARY: I just about got everything ready. Citizen's upstairs. He say he's ready to go.

ELI: He found the two pennies quick. She thought he'd be up there another two or three days.

BLACK MARY: He never stopped talking about it. He anxious to get his soul washed.

ELI: He must have done something real bad if he that anxious.

BLACK MARY: I don't know what he done. All I know he say he ready to go.

(*There is a knock on the door. Eli goes to answer it. Solly enters with his traveling bag.*)

ELI: Hey Solly. Come on in. Look like you ready to make that trip.

SOLLY: Yeah, I got to go get my sister. I just stopped to say good-bye.

ELI: Aunt Ester in her room. She fixing to take Citizen Barlow to the City of Bones. She say don't disturb her till she get ready.

SOLLY: Hey Black Mary. How much I owe you for writing me that letter?

BLACK MARY: You don't owe me nothing.

SOLLY: Naw. Naw. You got to take something. I appreciate it. I got to show my appreciation.

BLACK MARY: Give me a dime then.

SOLLY: I thought you was gonna say a nickel.

(Solly gives Black Mary a dime. She exits upstairs.)

I went up and saw Jefferson Culpepper. I told him I hope he was still here when I got back.

ELI: How old is Culpepper?

SOLLY: He ain't but seventy-two. I'm sixty-seven. He got five years on me. I told him he ain't eating right. He ain't ate right since his wife died.

ELI: Which way you going?

SOLLY: Down through West Virginia. I figure for the morning to catch me going through Wheeling. I might pick up some help on the road.

ELI: Stay away from the cities. It'll be easier. You get down to Georgia you can work your way over from there. I'd stay away from Birmingham if I were you.

SOLLY: They probably got that all blocked off.

(Citizen enters from upstairs.)

Hey Citizen Barlow. So you going to the City of Bones. I been to the City of Bones. It's something like you ain't never seen. A whole city a half mile by a half mile made of bones. All kind of bones. Leg bones. Arm bones. Head bones. It's a beautiful city. That's where I'm going when I die. I know where I'm going. Got Twelve Gates and it's got Twelve Gatekeepers. That's what I always wanted to be. A Keeper of the Gate!

CITIZEN: After I found my two pennies I come back past the mill and it had burnt down. It still had smoke coming out of it.

ELI: That's that tin. Most people don't know tin will burn. It will burn faster than paper. We learned that during the Civil War. I seen it happen.

CITIZEN: I still owe the mill some money.

SOLLY: You ain't got to worry about paying it.

CITIZEN: Making the people owe is worse than slavery.

SOLLY: Ain't nothing worse than slavery! I know. I was there. Dark was the night and cold was the ground. Look at that . . .

*(He hands Citizen a chain link.)*

That's my good luck piece. That piece of chain used to be around my ankle. They tried to chain me down but I beat them on that one. I say, I'm gonna keep this to remember by. I been lucky ever since. I beat them on a lot of things. I beat them when I got away. I had some people who helped me. They helped show me the way and looked out for me. I got all the way to Canada. There was eight of us. I was in Canada in 1857. I stood right there in Freedomland. That's what they called it. Freedomland. I asked myself, "What I'm gonna do?" I looked around. I didn't see nothing for me. I tried to feel different but I couldn't. I started crying. I hadn't cried since my daddy knocked me down for crying when I was ten years old. I breathed in real deep to taste the air. It didn't taste no different. The man what brought us over the border tried to talk with me. I just sat right down on the ground and started crying. I told him say, "I don't feel right." It didn't feel right being in freedom and my mama and all the other people still in bondage. Told him, "I'm going back with you." I stopped crying soon as I said that. I joined the Underground Railroad. Look at that . . .

*(Solly shows Citizen his stick.)*

That's sixty-two notches. That's sixty-two people I carried to freedom. I was looking to make it sixty-three when Abraham Lincoln come along and changed all that. Him and General Grant. I never did join the Union Army but I showed them where to go. I know all the routes. Me and Eli worked together many a time.

ELI: You needed to know all the routes if you wanted to get up to Canada. It wasn't easy. All right . . . we'd be down in the swamp and then we'd hear the call. (*Calls*) "Hoot. Hoot. Hoot."

SOLLY: Sound like an owl.

ELI: Three times: "Hoot. Hoot. Hoot."

SOLLY: Then we knew they had got through.

ELI: Sometime we'd hear the dogs right behind them. We'd make contact and get the runaways from the other conductor. See he just pass them on. Otherwise if he don't hook up with us he got to go out his section. He got to carry them farther. Maybe he don't know the woods as much as he do his own section. See, that make slower going . . . all the time the dogs after you. All the time. You got to keep going.

SOLLY: I was what we called the dragman. I'd guard the rear. You had to fight a lot of times. I done been bit nine times by dogs.

(*Solly shows Citizen his battle scars.*)

Look here . . . see that? A dog tried to tear my leg off one time. I got a big part of my arm missing. Tore out the muscle and everything. He was going for my throat. I told myself I was lucky. It was a good thing I found that pure otherwise I'd have to kill every dog I see.

ELI: All right . . . he hook up with us and pass them off and for the next two hundred miles they ours. It just go on like that till you in freedom.

SOLLY: Till you in Canada. You can't stay in the North. If you stay in the North you subject to end up back down South in slavery with a half a foot and waving one arm.

ELI: That's the way that went many a time. You got to leave the country to get freedom. You got to go up in Canada.

*(Eli gets a bottle of whiskey.)*

SOLLY: They got civilized people up there. I seen them. White as cotton. Got smiles on their faces. Shake your hand and say, "Welcome." I seen them. Don't never let nobody tell you there ain't no good white people. They got some good white people down here but they got to fight the law. In Canada they ain't got to fight the law. Down here it's a war.

ELI: It's a war and you always on the battlefield.

SOLLY: And the battlefield's bloody! The field of battle is *always* bloody. It can't be no other way.

ELI: The only thing you don't want to end up being the corpse. You don't want it to be your blood.

SOLLY: Ain't no sense in you getting mad 'cause it's rough out here. It's supposed to be rough. You ain't supposed to complain when you see some blood. I found out you could bleed and you didn't have to die. I said this is too good to be true! Since then I ain't never been afraid of losing some blood. I said they gonna have to kill me. I can give up some blood all day long if it'll keep coming back. Your blood is like a river it don't never stop till you dead. Life's got lots of comeback but death ain't got no comeback. That's the only way life have any meaning. Otherwise don't nothing count.

ELI: Come on, get you a drink. A man going to the City of Bones deserves a drink.

SOLLY: That boy too young to drink whiskey. You got to give it to him out a teaspoon.

CITIZEN: I drinks whiskey.

*(Eli pours each a drink of whiskey. Solly raises his glass in a toast.)*

SOLLY:
> So live, that when thy summons comes to join
> The innumerable caravan which moves
> To that mysterious realm, where each shall take
> His chamber in the silent halls of death,
> Thou go not, like the quarry-slave at night,
> Scourged to his dungeon, but, sustained and soothed
> By an unfaltering trust, approach thy grave
> Like one that wraps the drapery of his cough
> About him, and lies down to pleasant dreams.

*(They drink.)*

That's W. C. Bryant. I learned that poem when I was fourteen.

ELI:
> Thou go not, like the quarry-slave at night,
> Scourged to his dungeon, but, sustained and soothed
> By an *unfaltering* trust, approach thy grave
> Like one that wraps the drapery of his cough
> About him, and lies down to pleasant dreams.

You die by how you live.

SOLLY: They never made Emancipation what they say it was. People say, "Jesus turn the water into wine what you look like telling him it was the wrong kind?" Hell, maybe it is the wrong kind! If you gonna do it . . . do it right! They wave the law on one end and hit you with a billy club with the other. I told myself I can't just sit around and collect dog shit while the people drowning. The people drowning in sorrow and grief. That's a mighty big ocean. They got the law tied to their toe. Every time they try and swim the law pull them under. It's dangerous out here. People walking around hunting each other. If you ain't careful you could lose your eye or your arm. I seen that. I seen a man grab hold to a fellow and cut off his arm. Cut it off at the shoulder. He had to work at it a while . . . but he cut it clean off. The man looked down saw his arm gone and started crying. After that he more dangerous with that one arm than the other man is with two. He got less to lose. There's a lot of one-arm men walking around.

ELI: That's what Caesar can't understand. He can't see the people ain't got nothing to lose.

SOLLY: The trouble with Caesar is he think the people dumb. He think I'm dumb. The last person that thought that is walking around with one eye and half an ear. My mother used to say if you wanna teach an old dog new tricks you gonna need twice as many bones. Well, I got a pocketful of bones.

> I give you sugar for sugar
> And salt for salt . . .

*(Eli joins in:)*

SOLLY AND ELI:

> If you can't get along with me
> It's your own damn fault.

ELI: They fought the Civil War over the law and still ain't got it right.

SOLLY: You know about the Civil War? That was white people fighting and killing each other like you ain't never seen. I don't even think you can imagine that. White folks fighting each other over the Union.

ELI: They ain't got over it yet. They still fighting it. They still mad with each other.

SOLLY: I didn't know what the Union was until I saw the soldiers. They had on uniforms say they was Union soldiers and asked us could we help.

ELI: We knew every swamp hole. We knew all the back ways. We knew how to connect them up.

SOLLY: They say they needed that. Say the colored man got a right to life. Say they was fighting against slavery. I asked them what took them so long. My daddy fought against slavery all his life. They say, "We have guns." I turned and looked and they had great big old cannons. That's when I knew a whole lot of people was going to die when I looked at them cannons. They was real serious about it. I knew all them guns wasn't on account of me. I figure they was fighting for themselves. And if that would help them that would help us.

ELI: They never said *they* was gonna help us. They said the war was gonna help us. After that it be every man for himself.

SOLLY: I told them you get what's in it for you and I'll get what's in it for me. You get yours and I'll get mine and we'll settle the difference later. We still settling it.

(*Aunt Ester enters from her room.*)

AUNT ESTER: I see Solly out here making all that noise. What you doing sitting here?

SOLLY: I come to say good-bye. I'm on my way back down to Alabama.

AUNT ESTER: Mr. Citizen is going to the City of Bones. He's gonna need some help on the boat. Come on and help take Mr. Citizen to the City of Bones before you go.

SOLLY: My sister can't wait. If I'm going I got to go now.

AUNT ESTER: I know you want to help your sister. But I know you ain't gonna leave Mr. Citizen to fend for himself. That's not the Solly Two Kings I know.

64

SOLLY: All right. But I got to get on. I plan to be in Wheeling, West Virginia, by morning.

AUNT ESTER: Eli, put on the night light. Where's Black Mary? Get Black Mary. Come on, Mr. Citizen.

*(Aunt Ester hands him back the pennies.)*

You hold on to them two pennies, Mr. Citizen. You gonna need them. Jilson Grant was supposed to give you a piece of iron. You ain't got that. You got to go without it. That iron would have made you strong. That's what Samson had. His strength wasn't in his hair. He had a piece of iron that made him strong of heart and God found favor with him. You got to see if God find favor with you without that iron.

*(Solly hands Citizen his good luck chain link.)*

SOLLY: Here, put this piece of chain in your pocket. Now you got some iron. Jilson Grant ain't the only one got iron. That chain link brought me good luck many a time. Go on, put it in your pocket.

*(Black Mary enters from upstairs with European masks.)*

AUNT ESTER: You ready, Mr. Citizen?

CITIZEN: I'm ready.

AUNT ESTER: You see this boat, Mr. Citizen? It's called the *Gem of the Ocean.*

*(Aunt Ester hands him the paper boat made from the Bill of Sale.)*

You gonna take a ride on that boat. Come on, Black Mary. Solly. Eli. Mr. Citizen is going to the City of Bones. They gonna help us, Mr. Citizen. You can't never have enough help on the boat. Whatever happen you hold on to that boat. You hold on to that boat and everything will be all right. (*Singing:*)

Oh what a day

ELI, SOLLY AND BLACK MARY (*Singing*):
To go to the City of the Bones

AUNT ESTER (*Singing*):
Oh what a day

ELI, SOLLY AND BLACK MARY (*Singing*):
To go to the City of the Bones

AUNT ESTER (*Singing*):
We're going to that city

ELI, SOLLY AND BLACK MARY (*Singing*):
Going to the City of the Bones.

AUNT ESTER: Oh what a beautiful city, Mr. Citizen. It's a city like you ain't never seen. All the palaces a glittering with the light of the sun. (*Singing:*)

Oh what a day

ELI, SOLLY AND BLACK MARY (*Singing*):
Going to the City of the Bones.

(*Eli, Solly and Black Mary continue singing.*)

AUNT ESTER: You ever seen a boat, Mr. Citizen? A boat is made out of a lot of things. Wood and rope. The sails look like bedsheets blowing in the wind. They make a snap when the winds catch them. Wood and rope and iron.

The workmen with their hammers ringing. A boat is something. It takes a lot of men to make a boat. And it takes a lot of men to sail a boat. Them was some brave men. They left their family and didn't know if they was ever gonna see them again. They got on that boat and went out into the world. The world's a dangerous place, Mr. Citizen. It's got all kinds of harms in it. It take God to master the world. The world is a rough place. But there's gold out there in the world. There's good luck out there in the world. Them brave men went looking for it. Remember I told you you could take a ride on that boat? The wind catch up in them sails and you be off across the ocean. The wind will take you every which way. You need a strong arm to steer that boat. Don't you feel it, Mr. Citizen? Don't you feel that boat rocking? Just a rocking and a rocking. The wind blowing.

ELI: You got to watch out for that North wind.

SOLLY: That North wind got a mind of its own.

ELI: You can't reason with it.

SOLLY: The best you can do is try and outrun it. What you say, Black Mary?

BLACK MARY: It's like Satan. He's gonna have his way with you.

ELI: You got to figure out what to do.

AUNT ESTER: Just a rocking and a rocking. The wind blowing and the birds following behind that boat. They follow whenever it go. What is they following for, Mr. Citizen? The wind snapping them sails and the birds following. The birds following and singing and the fish swimming and the wind blowing—

(*Citizen gets up and makes a sudden move to balance himself.*)

CITIZEN: It's moving! The boat's moving! I feel it moving! The land . . . it's moving away.

AUNT ESTER: Do you see the sky?

CITIZEN: I see the sky.

AUNT ESTER: What color is it?

CITIZEN: It's blue color up close but farther along it's gray.

AUNT ESTER: That blue color is the skylight. That gray means trouble. That gray ain't supposed to be there. You hold on to that boat, Mr. Citizen. Whatever happen don't drop that boat. You hold on to that boat and everything will be all right. Do you see any stairs? If you see some stairs we can go down in the bottom. I been down in the bottom. Look and see if you see some stairs and we can go down in the bottom of the boat. If it rock too much we got to be careful.

CITIZEN: I see the stairs!

AUNT ESTER: Come on, Mr. Citizen, let's go down to the bottom of the boat. Be careful you don't fall.

CITIZEN: It's dark down here.

*(Solly, Eli and Black Mary begin singing:)*

SOLLY *(Singing)*:
    I got a home in the graveyard

ELI AND BLACK MARY *(Singing)*:
    Remember me

SOLLY *(Singing)*:
    Going down to the graveyard

ELI AND BLACK MARY *(Singing)*:
    Remember me

SOLLY *(Singing)*:
    Going down to the graveyard

ELI AND BLACK MARY (*Singing*):
    Remember me . . .

(*Eli, Black Mary and Solly continue singing.*)

CITIZEN: I hear people talking.
AUNT ESTER: What they saying, Mr. Citizen? Do you know
    what they saying?
CITIZEN: It sound like they singing.
AUNT ESTER: What they singing?
CITIZEN: They saying remember me.

(*Solly and Eli put on the European masks. They grab Citizen by
the arms and symbolically chain him to the boat.*)

I'm chained to the boat. Who chained me to the boat?
    Somebody help me.
AUNT ESTER: What about the people. Where are the people
CITIZEN: I don't see no people.
AUNT ESTER: Look close. Do you see any people? Look real
    close now.
CITIZEN: I see the people. They chained to the boat.
AUNT ESTER: Them people you seen got some powerful gods,
    Mr. Citizen. But they ain't on the boat with them. They
    don't know to call him on their own. God don't answer to
    no one man. God answer to the all. All the people. They
    need all the people. Them people you see is without God.
    When we get to the City of Bones I'm gonna show you
    what happen when all the people call on God with the one
    voice. God got beautiful splendors.
CITIZEN: They all look like me. They all got my face!

(*Citizen is terror-stricken to the point where he cannot breathe.
Black Mary comes to his aid.*)

BLACK MARY: Breathe deep. Take a deep breath. Look at me. Look at me. It's Black Mary. Do you remember me? Take my hand. It's me . . . Black Mary.

CITIZEN: The people . . . they chained to the boat.

BLACK MARY: Look at me, Mr. Citizen.

CITIZEN: Where am I?

BLACK MARY: You on the boat, Mr. Citizen. You going to the City of Bones.

CITIZEN: No! No!

*(Citizen throws down the boat. Immediately a storm comes up.)*

BLACK MARY: Your boat! You threw away your boat! Get your boat, Mr. Citizen!

AUNT ESTER: You can't get to the City of Bones without your boat, Mr. Citizen.

BLACK MARY: Get the boat!

AUNT ESTER: You can't go without your boat.

*(Citizen struggles against the storm to reach the boat. Masked Solly and masked Eli seize him before he reaches it. They symbolically brand and symbolically whip Citizen, then throw him into the hull of the boat. The hatch slams shut. Citizen finds himself alone.)*

CITIZEN: The stars. Where are the stars?

*(Citizen begins to sing an African lullaby to himself, a song his mother taught him. Then he is thirsty.)*

Water. I'm thirsty. I need some water.

AUNT ESTER: There is no water, Mr. Citizen. All you have is your chain link. The boat got into trouble. The water was lost overboard. The captain took what was left and set out in a small boat. He was a mean man. He was a selfish man.

The captain of the *Gem of the Ocean*. He took all the water and left the crew to die. But they survived. They followed the law of the sea. Life is above all. God raised it to a great height. Live, Mr. Citizen. Live to the fullest. You got a duty to life. So live, Mr. Citizen! Live!

*(Black Mary begins to sing "Twelve Gates to the City." Hearing the song, Citizen slowly unfolds from his fetal position. All is calm and peaceful. He stands up and looks to see the most beautiful sight he has ever seen. He has arrived at the City of Bones. He is awed by its beauty.)*

CITIZEN: There it is! It's made of bones! All the buildings and everything. Head bones and leg bones and rib bones. The streets look like silver. The trees are made of bones. The trees and everything made of bone.

AUNT ESTER: Do you see the people with their tongue on fire?

CITIZEN: I don't see no people.

*(Citizen suddenly sees a Gate.)*

AUNT ESTER: Do you see the Gate, Mr. Citizen?

CITIZEN: I see the Gate.

BLACK MARY: There are Twelve Gates, Mr. Citizen.

SOLLY: And Twelve Gatekeepers. You got to go through the Gatekeeper to get into the city.

AUNT ESTER: There are twelve ways to get into the city, Mr. Citizen. Do you have your two pennies? Where are your two pennies? If you have your two pennies you can go into the city. If you go into the city you can see my mother and all the people with their tongues on fire all glittering and dressed in their splendors. It's a sight like you ain't never seen.

CITIZEN: I got my two pennies!

AUNT ESTER: Then you got to pay the Gatekeeper your passage and he'll let you in the city. Do you see the Gatekeeper, Mr. Citizen?

CITIZEN: Yeah. Yeah I see him!

(*Solly steps before Citizen wearing the City of Bones mask and holding his stick.*)

AUNT ESTER: You got to tell him your name so he can write it down in the book. Then you got to pay your passage.
CITIZEN (*Excited, shouts*): Citizen Barlow. I got my two pennies!

(*Masked Solly holds out his stick, not letting Citizen pass.*)

He won't let me pass.
AUNT ESTER: Who is the Gatekeeper, Mr. Citizen? Is it somebody you know?

(*Citizen recoils in horror. He is struck dumb. He tries to speak but no words come out of his mouth.*)

What is it, Mr. Citizen? What do you see?
CITIZEN: The Gatekeeper . . . the Gatekeeper . . . it's Garret Brown the man who jumped in the river.
AUNT ESTER: You got to tell him, Mr. Citizen. The truth has to stand in the light. You got to get your soul washed.
CITIZEN: How come you didn't come out the water? You was supposed to come out the water.
AUNT ESTER: You got to tell him, Mr. Citizen. Otherwise you'll never be right with yourself. Peter denied Christ three times. You might not get lucky like Peter to have three chances. You got to tell him now.
CITIZEN: It was me. I done it. My name is Citizen Barlow. I stole the bucket of nails.

(*Masked Solly lets him pass.*)

The Gate's opening!

*(Overwhelmed by the sheer beauty of the city and the people with their tongues on fire, Citizen Barlow, now reborn as a man of the people, sits down and begins to cry. Solly removes his mask. The journey is over. Black Mary comes over and wipes Citizen's brow. She unbuttons his shirt and begins to wipe his chest.)*

Where am I?

BLACK MARY: You're in Aunt Ester's house. It's okay.

CITIZEN: I seen the city. I was on the boat. There was people on the boat.

BLACK MARY: It's okay now. You made it back. Everything gonna be all right.

*(Eli, Solly, Black Mary and Aunt Ester begin to sing in celebration:)*

AUNT ESTER *(Singing)*:
    You made it back

ELI, SOLLY AND BLACK MARY *(Singing)*:
    Back from the City of the Bones

AUNT ESTER *(Singing)*:
    You made it back

ELI, SOLLY AND BLACK MARY *(Singing)*:
    You came from the City of the Bones.

*(They continue singing in impromptu celebration. It is a rough but celebratory song. Then there is a loud knock on the door which shatters the mood of celebration. Aunt Ester motions for Eli to answer it. Eli answers the door. Caesar enters.)*

ELI: This a peaceful house.

CAESAR: Hey Eli. I see Solly here. Solly, you didn't know somebody seen you when you set fire to the mill. You didn't know that. You thought you was gonna get away with it. But you can't get away with nothing like that. You under arrest.

SOLLY: I'm under God's sky, motherfucker! That's what I'm under!

*(Solly whacks Caesar on the knee with his stick. Caesar grabs his leg and falls down. Solly runs out the door. Caesar gets up and hobbles to the door.)*

CAESAR *(Shouting after Solly)*: I'm gonna catch him. I'm gonna catch him if I have to chase him clean up into Canada. Busted me on my goddamn knee! You can't get away with nothing like that! Now I got to get *my* justice!

*(The lights go down on the scene.)*

SCENE 3

*The lights come up on Citizen and Black Mary in the kitchen. It is two hours later.*

CITIZEN: You believe Solly burned down the mill?

BLACK MARY: It don't make no difference. If Caesar catch him he'll kill him. That's what he talking about *his* justice. He'll kill him and won't even think nothing of it. He got a streak in him like that. If he capture him alive he gonna bring him in dead. Ain't nothing I can do about it. Ain't nothing nobody can do about it.

CITIZEN: I don't believe he can catch him 'cause he don't know where he going. Solly used to running. He's probably halfway to Alabama by now. I wouldn't worry about Solly if I was you. Solly can take care of himself. We talking about Solly Two Kings.

BLACK MARY: We talking about Caesar Wilks too. I ain't never know him to give up on nothing. Once he got it fixed in his mind to do something he don't let nothing stop him.

*(Pause as Citizen takes in the woman before him.)*

CITIZEN: You got on that blue dress. I met this gal at a dance one time had on a blue dress. She had on a blue dress and she had her hair slicked back. Her mouth made her face look pretty. She was dancing and she had tears in her eyes. I asked her why she was crying. She said she was lonesome. I told her I couldn't fix that but if she wanted somebody to walk her home after the dance I'd walk her. See that she got home safe. She thanked me and went on crying. Say she felt better, and after the dance I could walk her home since I was going that way. She had a good time dancing with some of the other men. I danced with her some more. She was smiling but she still had tears in her eyes. After the dance I walked her home. I seen at the dance that she had a nice way about her. When she was walking home she put her hand in mine. She asked me did I want to stay the night. I told her yes. I told her I was at the dance looking for a woman. She asked me why didn't I tell her, we could have saved each other some time. I woke up in the morning and she was laying there crying. I didn't ask her about it. I didn't try and stop her. I lay there a while trying to figure out what to do. I ended up holding her in my arms. She started crying some more. I held her a while and then I left. I said good-bye to her and started walking away. She was standing in the door. I looked back and she was standing so she fit right in the middle of the door. I couldn't see if she was crying. She kind of waved at me. I got a little further on and turned and looked back and she was still there. Look like she had got smaller like she might have sat down in the doorway. That's what it looked like to me. I can still see her standing there. Had a green door and I can see her standing in it. I don't know what happened to her. I'd like to look on her face again. Just to know that she all right and if she stopped crying. If I could see her face I believe that would be enough.

BLACK MARY: Maybe you'll get the chance. What you gonna tell her if you see her again?

CITIZEN: I don't know. Sometimes I lay awake at night when I be lonely and ask myself what I would say to her. Sometimes I tell her to stop being lonely. I tell her it's something she doing to herself. But then I'm laying there lonely too and I have to ask myself was it something I was doing to myself? I don't know. I ain't lonely now. I ain't got no woman but I still don't feel lonely. I feel all filled up inside. That's something I done to myself. So maybe I did make myself lonely.

BLACK MARY: You got to be right with yourself before you can be right with anybody else.

CITIZEN: That's what I'd tell her! I believe she was looking for somebody else to make her right with herself. That's why she was crying.

(Aunt Ester enters from her room.)

AUNT ESTER: Mr. Citizen, listen to what I tell you now. Rutherford Selig should be heading upriver by now. He go through Little Haiti and then he cross over the river to go to Scotch Bottom before he go to Hazelwood. You got to catch him before he cross the river. He sells pots and pans. Look for a wagon by the river with pots and pans. That's Rutherford Selig. Tell him Aunt Ester needs him. Ask him to come right away. Then you come back with him. Be careful. If Caesar see you he'll follow you. Hurry now, the time ain't long. If Rutherford Selig get across the river you can't catch him. Ask him to come right away.

CITIZEN: I'll catch him.

AUNT ESTER: You look just like my Junebug. You old rascal you! You be careful. Go in prayer.

*(Citizen exits.)*

Black Mary, fix up a plate of whatever you got and bring it in the room. Draw that shade. Bring me that plate and let me know when Selig comes. You got that stove too hot. Damp it down. You be done burnt down the place.

BLACK MARY: It's down already.

AUNT ESTER: It's too hot. Damp it down! Take some of that wood off that fire.

BLACK MARY: You need fire to cook with. How else the food gonna get done?

AUNT ESTER: Turn it down!

BLACK MARY: Here! You cook it! You turn it down! I can't do everything the way you want me to. I'm not you. You act like there ain't no other way to do nothing. I got my own way of doing things. I like the fire high. That's the way I cook. You like it down. That's the way you cook. If you ain't cooking you ain't got nothing to say about it. All you got to worry about is the eating.

AUNT ESTER: I just say the fire's too high.

BLACK MARY: It's been three years now I can't do nothing to satisfy you. I may as well lay down somewhere and forget about it. You got something to say about everything. Turn the fire down. Wash the greens in the other pot. Shake that flour off that chicken. Tuck in the corners of the sheets. That too much starch. That ain't enough salt. I'm tired of it! Your way ain't always the best way. I got my own way and that's the way I'm doing it. If I stay around here I'm doing it my own way.

AUNT ESTER: What took you so long?

77

*(Aunt Ester turns and exits into her room. The lights go down on the scene.)*

## SCENE 4

*The lights come up on Eli, standing looking out the window. Black Mary is in the kitchen. Eli sees Selig's wagon.*

ELI: Here he comes now.

*(Eli heads to the back door and opens it. Citizen and Selig enter.)*

Come on in, Selig. Aunt Ester's waiting on you.

SELIG: Good thing Citizen caught up with me. They got all the roads blocked off. They say they looking for whoever burnt down the mill. They say they know who done it. They won't let anybody cross the river down in Scotch Bottom.

*(Aunt Ester enters from her room.)*

AUNT ESTER: How you doing, Mr. Selig? I thank you for coming. I need you to do me a favor. God is a good worker and he works all kind of ways in the world. The Bible say he rewards those who do just works. I need you to do me a favor. Caesar might catch you and if he catch you I can't say what the matter will be.

SELIG: I ain't never known you to be on the wrong side of anything. I ain't scared of Caesar.

AUNT ESTER: I need you to carry Solly downriver. Caesar looking for him. Say he burnt down the mill. I don't know whether he did or not. Sometimes them ain't the right questions.

*(Solly enters from Aunt Ester's room.)*

SOLLY: Yeah, I burned it down! The people might get mad but freedom got a high price. You got to pay. No matter what it cost. You got to pay. I didn't mind settling up the difference after the war. But I didn't know they was gonna settle like this. I got older I see where I'm gonna die and everything gonna be the same. I say well at least goddamn it they gonna know I was here! The people gonna know about Solly Two Kings!

SELIG: I got my wagon out back.

AUNT ESTER *(To Solly)*: If Caesar catches you he'll kill you. You know that?

SOLLY: He gonna have to catch me first.

*(Eli is watching out the window.)*

CITIZEN: I'll go with you. He gonna have to catch both of us.

SOLLY: You on the battlefield now.

ELI: You belong to the band.

SOLLY *(To Aunt Ester)*: I'm gonna try and get to Alabama. I don't know what's gonna happen. If he get me I want you to come and find me and say a prayer for me. You got some powerful prayer. You special, Ester. I'll always think of you that way. You don't have to bring me no flowers. Just come and say a prayer for me.

AUNT ESTER: You pretty special yourself, Solly Two Kings, you old rascal you.

*(Aunt Ester kisses Solly on the cheek.*
*Citizen looks at Black Mary.)*

CITIZEN: Black Mary, is you right with yourself? 'Cause if you is I believe when I come back from down Alabama I'd come by and see you. If I was still right with myself. Then maybe we could be right with each other.

*(Black Mary looks at him a long moment.)*

BLACK MARY: You stop on by, Mr. Citizen. You stop on by anytime you want.

*(Citizen gives her a strong embrace.)*

You be careful. It's a big world out there and there's lots of harms in it. May God bless you everywhere you go.

ELI: Caesar's coming down the street!

*(Solly, at the back door, turns to Aunt Ester for a quick embrace. Aunt Ester pushes him out the door.)*

AUNT ESTER: Go!

*(Solly exits. Aunt Ester takes Citizen's hands and pushes him out the back door.)*

Go in peace! May God bless you!

*(Citizen exits. There is a knock on the front door. Selig takes a seat at the table. Eli answers the door. Caesar enters.)*

ELI: This a peaceful house, Caesar. It's right there on the door. 1839 Wylie.

CAESAR: I come in peace, Eli. But I come in the name of the law. The law's got certain rights. That's what keeps the peace. Without that you'd have run amok.

*(He sees Selig.)*

Hey, Selig.

SELIG: How you doing, Caesar? Black Mary, I'll have that fourteen-inch frying pan for you next week.

BLACK MARY: Bring me a dustpan too. I need a new dustpan.

SELIG: Aunt Ester, I'll see you the next time. I got to get on.

AUNT ESTER: You take care, Mr. Selig. May God bless you and keep you in the palm of his hand.

CAESAR: If you going downriver you got to cross at Braddock. All the other roads are blocked.

SELIG: Okay, thanks Caesar.

*(Selig exits out the back door.)*

AUNT ESTER: Sit on down there, Mr. Caesar. I'm getting so I can't hardly move no more. I don't know what it is. My joints don't move right. If this keep up I'm gonna have to send for the doctor.

CAESAR: Aunt Ester, I got a warrant here . . .

AUNT ESTER: I see you got a piece of paper. I got a piece of paper too. Black Mary, get my piece of paper over there. Sit on down there, Mr. Caesar, I want to show you something.

*(Black Mary takes the paper boat out of the drawer and hands it to Aunt Ester. She unfolds it and hands it back to Black Mary.)*

Give that to Caesar, let him take a look at it.

*(Black Mary hands Caesar the paper.)*

Tell me how much that piece of paper's worth, Mr. Caesar.

CAESAR *(Reading)*: "Know all men by these present that I, William J. Ogburn of the County of Guilford . . . State of North Carolina, have this day sold and delivered . . . to Issac Thatcher . . . a Negro slave girl named Ester, twelve years five months old . . . for the sum of $607: the right and title to said girl . . . I warrant and defend now and forever to be sound and healthy." This a Bill of Sale.

AUNT ESTER: It say on there Ester. That's a Bill of Sale for Ester Tyler. That's me. Now you tell me how much it's worth, Mr. Caesar.

CAESAR: I wouldn't give you ten cents for it.

AUNT ESTER: Then how much you think your paper's worth? You see, Mr. Caesar, you can put the law on the paper but that don't make it right. That piece of paper say I was property. Say anybody could buy or sell me. The law say I needed a piece of paper to say I was a free woman. But I didn't need no piece of paper to tell me that. Do you need a piece of paper, Mr. Caesar?

CAESAR: These ain't slavery times no more, Miss Tyler. You living in the past. All that done changed. The law done changed and I'm a custodian of the law. Now you know, Miss Tyler, you got to have rule of law otherwise there'd be chaos. Nobody wants to live in chaos. Now I got a warrant . . .

BLACK MARY: This house is sanctuary! It's been sanctuary for a long time. You know that. Everybody know that. This is 1839 Wylie Avenue.

CAESAR: I don't know nothing about no sanctuary. Somebody break the law I got to arrest them. Don't care where they at. 1839 Wylie Avenue ain't no different than any other house.

BLACK MARY: 1839 Wylie Avenue is a house of sanctuary. It ain't up to you to decide. The Bible say, "A place of refuge shall be given unto you and whosoever seeketh counsel therein shall he be made also clean, for I have given unto the master of that abode a place above the law, for the law is a punisher of men, and I seeketh their redemption."

CAESAR: I got my Bible right here.

*(He takes out a small handbook.)*

"The Penal Code of the Commonwealth of Pennsylvania. Section 14, Number 7409: Aiding and Abetting." Now,

Alfred Jackson is a fugitive from the law and anybody harboring him is aiding and abetting. They breaking the law. I'm trying to be nice about this. But I got a warrant here signed by Judge Homer S. Brown, duly elected official under the laws of the Commonwealth of the State of Pennsylvania. I'm just trying to do my job.

AUNT ESTER: You think you a strong man, Mr. Caesar. But you got that gun. That tell me all I need to know. I see that gun and I know the truth. A man will come and stand and look at the stars. That gun can't take that away from him. You can shoot him but sooner or later somebody gonna come and stand in the same spot. He's gonna come and stand and *count* the stars. Black Mary, put that pot on and bring Mr. Caesar some tea.

CAESAR: I ain't got time for no tea. I'm here to serve a warrant. I got a warrant here for the arrest of Ester Tyler for interfering with the administration of justice and aiding and abetting Alfred Jackson, a fugitive of the law. Them is serious crimes, Miss Tyler. You're under arrest.

AUNT ESTER: You a scoundrel, Mr. Caesar. Black Mary, bring me my shawl.

*(Eli gets out the shotgun, cocks it and points it at Caesar.)*

ELI: You don't need no shawl. You ain't going nowhere. I told you when you came in here this a peaceful house.

CAESAR: See, you breaking the law right now. I'm gonna overlook that, Eli. Aunt Ester know I got to do my job.

AUNT ESTER: It's all right, Eli.

*(Eli immediately uncocks the gun and drops it to his side.)*

Black Mary, bring me my shawl.

*(Black Mary brings Aunt Ester her shawl. Aunt Ester ties a scarf around her head and goes and stands by the door.)*

I'm ready, Mr. Caesar.

CAESAR: I'm just doing my job, Eli. The people wouldn't have it any other way.

*(Caesar takes Aunt Ester by the arm and they exit. The lights go down on the scene.)*

## SCENE 5

*The lights come up on Black Mary. Eli and Aunt Ester enter. Aunt Ester, without saying a word, goes to her room. Black Mary looks at Eli questioningly.*

ELI: She tired. You'd be tired too if you went through what she been through.

BLACK MARY: How much was the bond?

ELI: A hundred dollars.

BLACK MARY: When does she have to go to court?

ELI: The judge say she got to be back down there next Monday.

BLACK MARY: I kept the food warm. You hungry? You want something to eat?

ELI: Naw, I ain't hungry.

BLACK MARY: I'm gonna see if Aunt Ester want anything.

*(Black Mary exits into Aunt Ester's room. Eli, tired, sits in the chair and closes his eyes. There is a sound from upstairs. Eli is startled. He goes and gets his shotgun and waits beside the stairs, out of view from any intruder, his gun pointed. Citizen enters from the stairs on his way to the back door.)*

CITIZEN: Caesar shot Solly. Selig out the back.

*(Citizen exits out the back. Eli immediately starts to follow. Black Mary enters.)*

ELI: Solly's been shot.

*(Eli starts to exit out the back door as Citizen and Selig, supporting Solly on each side, bring him in the house. Solly collapses on the floor. He slips in and out of consciousness and occasionally mutters, "So live."*
    *Aunt Ester enters.)*

Caesar shot Solly.

AUNT ESTER: Put him on the table. Eli, see if you can get him up on the table. Black Mary, put on some water. And get them clean cloths out the cupboard.

*(Aunt Ester and Black Mary begin to work urgently at treating the wound, trying to stop the flow of blood. For Aunt Ester it is an old, old, unwelcome visitation.)*

SELIG: We got through the road block without any trouble. We got all the way to West Virginia. Solly seen I had a can of kerosene in the wagon. He seen that kerosene and he told me to turn around and take him back to the jail.

CITIZEN *(To Eli)*: Solly say he was gonna get him another boat and some more men. I don't know what he meant by that. But the people that were arrested during the riot at the mill he say he was gonna bust them out of jail. Say he didn't feel right being free and the rest of the people in bondage.

SELIG: We never got as far as the jail. Caesar seen the wagon and started shooting.

CITIZEN: He shot Solly in the chest. It looks like it pretty bad.

ELI: Solly's been shot, clubbed, bit by dogs, chained, whipped, knocked down, and still raise more hell than any two men I know.

CITIZEN: I got his chain link. He say he used that for good luck. I keep thinking if he had it everything would have turned out all right.

ELI: I know Solly. He ain't going before his time. And . . . I don't believe it's his time.

(*Aunt Ester and Black Mary begin to sing:*)

AUNT ESTER AND BLACK MARY (*Singing*):
> Now is a needy time
> Now is a needy time

(*Eli joins in the song:*)

AUNT ESTER, BLACK MARY AND ELI (*Singing*):
> Oh, now is a needy time
> Oh, now is a needy time
> O Lord won't you come by here
>
> Now is a needy time
> Now is a needy time
> Oh, now—

(*They break off their singing individually as they realize that Solly is dead. There is a moment of silence in recognition. Aunt Ester breaks the silence.*)

AUNT ESTER: Black Mary, go get the cloth. Mr. Citizen, you still got your two pennies. Solly's gonna need them to pay his passage.

(*Citizen steps forward, takes his two pennies, places them in Solly's hand, closes it and lays Solly's hand on his chest. Black Mary enters with the ceremonial shawl and helps Aunt Ester place it around her shoulders. Selig begins a procession, then*) *approaches the body. Paying his respects, he takes off his hat. Black Mary follows and kisses Solly on the cheek. Eli pays his respects and then delivers the eulogy:)*

ELI: They laid him low. Put him in the cold ground. David and Solomon. Two kings in the cold ground. Solly never did find his freedom. He always believed he was gonna find it. The battlefield is always bloody. Blood here. Blood there. Blood over yonder. Everybody bleeding. Everybody been cut and most of them don't even know it. But they bleeding just the same. It's all you can do sometime just to stand up. Solly stood up and walked.

He lived in truth and he died in truth. He died on the battlefield. You live right you die right.

*(There is a loud rapping at the door. Eli pushes Citizen toward Aunt Ester's room. After Citizen is hid, Eli goes and answers the door. Caesar enters. He has come to arrest Citizen. Caesar takes in the scene.)*

CAESAR: Where's that Barlow fellow?

SELIG: That other fellow ran off. I believe he was going to Philadelphia.

CAESAR: Selig, I see where they hijacked your wagon. I'm gonna need to get a statement from you. You told me you was going downriver but when I seen your wagon I knew something was wrong. Don't worry I'm gonna get that Barlow fellow too. He can't get far. We got all the hospitals on the lookout. We got all the roads blocked. If he try to go downriver we got him. If he try to go upriver we got him.

*(Caesar goes over and looks at Solly.)*

He thought he was gonna get away with it. You can't get away with nothing like that. I say good riddance.

BLACK MARY: Caesar, I gave you everything. Even when I didn't have to give you. I made every way for you. I turned my eyes away. I figured if I didn't see it I couldn't hold fault. If I held fault I couldn't hold on to my love for you. But now you standing in the light and I can't turn away no more. I remember you when you was on the other side of the law. That's my brother. The one selling hoecakes off the back of a wagon. The one that helped Mrs. Robinson and the kids when nobody else would. That's my brother. The one who used to get out of bed to take me to school. The one who believed everybody had the same right to life . . . the same right to whatever there was in life they could find useful. That's my brother. I don't know who you are. But you not my brother. You hear me, Caesar? You not my brother.

*(Caesar is stunned by this declaration. He crosses to the door, turns and looks back at Black Mary, then raises himself to his full height and exits.)*

AUNT ESTER *(Singing)*:
> Come on, come on
> Let's go to burying ground

*(Citizen enters from Aunt Ester's room.)*

> Come on, come on

ELI AND BLACK MARY *(Singing)*:
> Let's go to burying ground
> Come on, come on
> Let's go to burying ground
> Come on, come on

ELI (*Singing*):
> The hammer keeps a ringing

AUNT ESTER AND BLACK MARY (*Singing*):
> On somebody's coffin

ELI (*Singing*):
> The hammer keeps a ringing

AUNT ESTER AND BLACK MARY (*Singing*):
> On somebody's coffin
> Over on the new burying ground.

> (*Citizen takes off his coat. He puts on Solly's coat and hat and takes Solly's stick. He discovers the letter from Solly's sister in the hat. Eli pours a drink and raises it in a toast.*)

ELI: So live.

> (*Without a word Citizen turns and exits. The lights go down on the scene.*)

END OF PLAY

# August Wilson

## April 27, 1945–October 2, 2005

August Wilson authored *Gem of the Ocean, Joe Turner's Come and Gone, Ma Rainey's Black Bottom, The Piano Lesson, Seven Guitars, Fences, Two Trains Running, Jitney, King Hedley II* and *Radio Golf*. These works explore the heritage and experience of African Americans, decade by decade, over the course of the twentieth century. Mr. Wilson's plays have been produced at regional theaters across the country, on Broadway and throughout the world. In 2003, Mr. Wilson made his professional stage debut in his one-man show *How I Learned What I Learned*.

Mr. Wilson's work garnered many awards, including the Pulitzer Prize for *Fences* (1987) and *The Piano Lesson* (1990); a Tony Award for *Fences*; Great Britain's Olivier Award for *Jitney*; and eight New York Drama Critics Circle awards for *Ma Rainey's Black Bottom, Fences, Joe Turner's Come and Gone, The Piano Lesson, Two Trains Running, Seven Guitars, Jitney* and *Radio Golf*. Additionally, the cast recording of *Ma Rainey's Black Bottom* received a 1985 Grammy Award, and Mr. Wilson received a 1995 Emmy Award nomination for his screenplay adaptation of *The Piano Lesson*. Mr. Wilson's early works include the one-act plays: *The Janitor, Recycle, The Coldest Day of the Year, Malcolm X, The Homecoming* and the musical satire *Black Bart and the Sacred Hills*.

Mr. Wilson received many fellowships and awards, including Rockefeller and Guggenheim fellowships in play-writing, the Whiting Writers Award and the 2003 Heinz Award. He was awarded a 1999 National Humanities Medal by the President of the United States, and received numerous honorary degrees from colleges and universities, as well as the only high school diploma ever issued by the Carnegie Library of Pittsburgh.

He was an alumnus of New Dramatists, a member of the American Academy of Arts and Sciences, a 1995 inductee into the American Academy of Arts and Letters, and on October 16, 2005, Broadway renamed the theater located at 245 West 52nd Street: The August Wilson Theatre. In 2007, he was posthumously inducted into the Theater Hall of Fame.

Mr. Wilson was born and raised in the Hill District of Pittsburgh, and lived in Seattle at the time of his death. He is survived by two daughters, Sakina Ansari and Azula Carmen Wilson, and his wife, costume designer Constanza Romero.